The Why & How
of Bible Translation

New, Expanded Edition

Blessings!

Jack

Ps. 119:105

Jack Popjes

What You Could Learn from This Book

- You already know the names of the very first Bible translators, Matthew, Mark, Luke and John who translated the words of Jesus from Aramaic into Greek, a completely different, unrelated language and culture.
- Learn why Greek, Hebrew, and Latin are *not* holy languages and why every language of the world is fully capable of expressing the truths of God's Word.
- Discover why in some instances Mark and Luke did *not* quote Jesus exactly as Matthew did, and why today's translators may need to follow Mark and Luke's example.
- Find out why it is sometimes essential for translators to state explicitly in the target language what is merely implied in the original Greek text.
- Understand how illustrative metaphors and similes must be translated, and the critical difference between the *form* and the *function* of a metaphor.
- Discover that translating from one language to another is relatively easy compared to translating from one culture to another.
- Learn why ignorance of the basic nature of language and culture is the reason for most criticism of Bible translation.
- Find out why support for Bible translation would skyrocket among Christians if linguistics were taught as widely as biology, chemistry or physics.
- Understand why no pastor and no missionary anywhere in the world can do any lasting ministry without the Word of God in the language of the people to whom they minister.
- Learn the Church's one basic, critical task still to be completed before the return of Christ.

The Why and How of Bible Translation
What Every Christian Should Know
But Few Do, Very Few

New, Expanded Edition

Jack Popjes

Cover Design and Development:Aaron Parker & Micayla Jones

Formatting by Wild Seas Formatting

(http://www.WildSeasFormatting.com)

ISBN - 13: 978-1985166967

ISBN - 10: 1985166968

Table of Contents

Author's Preface

My Linguistic Background

For twelve years, as I grew up in the Netherlands I was surrounded by the sound of various languages. Dutch was the common language, but during my early years, I also heard plenty of German from the occupying soldiers. My father and mother grew up in the northern province of Friesland and invariably spoke Frisian to each other when they wanted to hide something from me—a huge incentive for me to learn to understand Frisian and not let them know I understood! I learned to sing some hymns in English in grade school and was exposed to French and given some lessons by an aunt who spoke it fluently.

I read voraciously in Dutch until I was twelve years old. Then our family immigrated to Canada, and I learned English by reading comics from the magazine rack in the drugstore. After a few months, I got a library card and read books in English, going through them as fire goes through kindling. Since then I have become proficient in two more languages – Portuguese and Canela

My Bible Translation Background

In Bible school, I compared my Dutch *Statenvertaling Bijbel* with my English *King James Version* Bible and noticed many differences even though both translations were translated from the same source text at about the same time in the early 1600s. These differences piqued my interest in the principles and techniques of Bible translation.

After completing three years of biblical training, my wife and I began linguistic training in 1964, joined Wycliffe Bible Translators, moved to Brazil in 1966 and began research work with the Canela people in 1968, learning their culture and unwritten language. In 1990, we left them with literacy materials in Canela, trained literacy teachers and a translation of a 750-

page partial Bible, one-third being Old Testament, two-thirds New Testament.

Why I Wrote and Compiled This Book

This book of story-based articles grew out of both our personal experience and that of our colleagues in Brazil who shared this challenging work with us. During each furlough, I spoke about our translation ministry at least one-hundred times in churches, Bible schools, and missions conferences. After completing our translation ministry, I was engaged in missions speaking ministry for many years, traveling extensively to speak at events throughout Canada, the United States and a dozen other countries.

As I interacted with Bible-believing Christians, experienced pastors, and even highly educated theologians and professors, I was shocked at the profound ignorance I found among them about languages, cultures, and the principles and techniques of Bible translation. I sought to correct this ignorance through my story-laden speeches, and later through my weekly story-based blog posts.

What This Book Is Not, and What it Is

This book is not a systematic theology of Bible translation. It is not a logically presented argument seeking to convince the reader. Instead, it is a series of stories or story-based articles that leave the readers to draw their own conclusions, much as Jesus told His parables, leaving His hearers to think through what they had heard.

New Expanded Edition

This book was published as an ebook in 2013 having only 29 articles. This edition is published both in print and as an ebook and has been expanded to 52 articles

Acknowledgements

Every article in this book was published as a blog post on my blog InSights & OutBursts (www.jackpopjes.com) after it was critiqued by my wife, Josephine, and corrected by my daughter, Leanne. Many thanks to all the blog readers who commented and whose suggestions I often incorporated for this collection.

Section One: Why the Bible Must be Translated

Jesus and the Giant Scissors

When God chose to reveal Himself to people, He decided to use human language, and in so doing, opened a huge can of worms.

The problem with languages is that they are alive. Just like living, growing trees, it is the nature of languages to grow, develop and change over time. It should be no surprise, therefore, that translations of the God-revealing Bible done hundreds of years ago are more difficult to understand now than when they were first translated.

The Bible Reading That Made Me Laugh

When I was a little boy growing up in Holland, most church-going Dutch people had the custom of reading some Scripture after the main meal. Papa read from the Bible in an old translation, completed nearly 350 years before. Naturally the modern Dutch we spoke at home and in school was markedly different.

One day, Papa read about Jesus preaching to a giant pair of scissors. The picture that popped into my mind was so funny I laughed out loud. The 1619 Dutch word for crowd was *schaare*, which sounded to me like the word *schaar*, the modern word for scissors and nothing like *menigte*, the modern Dutch word for crowd. Thus, I understood *groote schaare* to be a giant pair of scissors. After scolding me for laughing, Papa explained the meaning of the obsolete term.

Not only do all languages tend to change, but also the more a language is used, the faster it changes. Since more people, in more countries, speak some variety of English than any other language, it is no surprise that English is changing fast.

That is one reason translators keep churning out so many

different translations and paraphrased versions of the Bible in English. Critics contend that there are too many already, and they may have a point, but translations do need to be upgraded to keep up with changes in the language that people are speaking.

Outdated Language Often Results in Wrong Understanding and Can be Funny

A six-year-old recited the Lord's Prayer at a church service this way: "And forgive us our trash passes, as we forgive those who pass trash against us."

After reading the story of the coming of the Holy Spirit at Pentecost to her Sunday school class, a teacher had children draw pictures of the story. Most of them drew people with little flames dancing above their heads. But one boy drew a group of people packed in a room, into which a car was also jammed. The vehicle was a Honda, apparently, since the little "H" symbol showed clearly on the hood.

"Why do you have a car in the picture?" the teacher asked him "There is no car in the story.

"Yes, there is," he replied. "You read, 'They were all with one Accord, in one place'."

The Kaska and the KJV

My earliest cross-cultural missions experience was as a 21-year-old Bible College student in the Yukon, in north-western Canada. For several months my ministry partner and I held church services in a village of indigenous people. They spoke their own Kaska language among themselves and English with us.

I preached and taught informally, both answering and asking questions during my sermons. I read to them from the King James Authorized Version. From the questions I fielded, I was convinced the Kaska people did not understand it. How could they, since modern English was not their heart language, and the KJV translation was, at that time, 350 years old?

My colleague, not being an immigrant who had needed to learn English on the fly, had never experienced the frustration of hearing words and not understanding them. He just wanted to read the old King James Bible slowly, clearly and expressively, over and over again, and believed the Kaska speakers would eventually understand it. I doubted it then and doubt it even more strongly now.

The Amsterdam Declaration

Four decades later, I was part of a team promoting Bible translation at Amsterdam 2000, a convention of the Billy Graham Evangelistic Association attended by 12,000 evangelists from all over the world. Scores of theologians worked to develop the "Amsterdam Declaration." It clearly states the importance of Bible translation.

The declaration states, "We must proclaim and disseminate the Holy Scriptures in the heart language of all those we are called to evangelize and disciple. We pledge ourselves to…remove all known language and cultural barriers to a clear understanding of the gospel on the part of our hearers."

This is a far cry from repeatedly, clearly and expressively reading a Bible translation that is 350 years out of date to a group of people who barely understand modern English. Faith comes by hearing—the hearing of the Word of God. This biblical truth implies hearing it with understanding, which means that we must hear or read the Bible in the language that we know best.

It is great to know that speakers of more than 3,300 languages can hear or read at least some of the Bible with good understanding. No more Jesus preaching to giant scissors.

What's more, Bible translation programs—many staffed by nationals who are translating into their own language—are currently active in nearly 2,600 more languages. That adds up to 5,900 languages with either an existing translation of some Scriptures or an ongoing translation project.

There is good progress being made in dealing with the can of worms that is the diversity of human language, even though 114 million speakers of 1636 languages are still not able to hear or read God's message to them in their own language.

They continue to wait for the Word of God to be translated into their own language.

~~~~~~~~~~

A Fair and Simple Question

"If the Bible is already published in the national language, why don't you Wycliffe folk just teach the indigenous peoples living in that country the national language?" a young businessman asked.

I had just answered a question from someone in the group about Bible translation problems and how my wife and I had struggled to solve them when we worked as Wycliffe Bible translators among the Canela people of Brazil. It was not the first time someone had asked me this follow-up question. It's a simple question and a fair one, but requires some complex answers.

Sometimes I ask a counter-question: "What do you think is easier? For a college educated team of linguists, literacy specialists and Bible translators to learn a language, translate the Bible into it, and teach the people to read their own language, or to teach thousands of illiterate people to read in the national language which most don't understand at all and of which the rest have only minimal understanding?

More Explanation

But more explanation is usually needed. First of all, Wycliffe does move people towards being able to speak, read and write in the national language. But we don't do it by disrespecting the indigenous people's own language. Often the indigenous language has never been written, and the speakers are unable to read or write in any language. So we start by developing a writing system, using letters and symbols as close to the national language as possible. We then teach people to read and write in their own language. Eventually, when they interact with speakers of the national language and begin speaking it, it is relatively easy for them to learn to read and write in the national language.

Years ago, the official policies of most national educational systems belittled and denigrated the indigenous languages people spoke at home and attempted to teach everything, even basic things like reading, directly in the national language. First Nations adults in Canada have told me that as young people in school they were physically punished when they were caught speaking their native language. Except in the case of very bright and highly motivated students, the learning results were usually rather negative.

Related Languages

In the context of learning to read in a second language, I am often asked about French immersion teaching programs for English speaking grade one students. My parents spoke Frisian at home and learned to speak and read Dutch when they went to school. It was a successful language learning immersion program since Frisian and Dutch are related languages. My wife spoke Plautdietsch, also called Low German, at home and learned English and reading when she started school. Again, this was successful because Plautdietsch and English are related languages. The same with French and English, the languages are related and have many cognates—words similar in shape and meaning that are easily recognized and learned. These European languages are simply branches on the same linguistic tree.

I grew up speaking and reading Dutch. When I arrived in Canada as a twelve-year-old immigrant, it took only a couple of weeks in school before I could read English quite fluently. I certainly didn't understand everything I read, but that improved as I learned to speak English. The same thing happened years later when Jo and I moved to Brazil, and we were soon reading

Portuguese, also a related language.

But learning to speak Ramkokamekra-Canela was a long process. This indigenous language was not just a different branch on the same linguistic tree. It was a different tree, in a different forest—as different from European languages as a coconut palm is from an apple tree.

Unrelated Languages

Now imagine an English speaking first grader starting school where the teacher taught in an utterly unrelated African language like Somali, and she had to learn to read in this completely unknown, unrelated language that looks like this:

"Qolobaa calankeed, waa ceynoo." *Any nation's flag, bears its own color.* The first line of the Somali national anthem.

To teach an indigenous people group to speak and read a completely unrelated national language would be as difficult as teaching English speaking first graders to learn to read in Somali.

In the same way, it is just as hard for the thousands of indigenous illiterate people who live in Somalia but do not speak Somali. There are thousands of people groups, speaking their own, often unwritten languages, which live in countries where the national language is completely unrelated to the languages they speak.

This is the first part of the answer. But there is another aspect. A story from the early days of the Wycliffe organization has an indigenous person ask a missionary, "If your God is so great, how come He can't speak our language?"

~~~~~~~~~~

Eight Reasons Why We Translate the Bible

Teaching illiterate persons to read in a language they do not understand and see no reason to learn, is like trying to motivate people to visit an attic they have no desire to visit, using a ladder from which the bottom three rungs are missing.

Last week's post described the work of replacing those missing rungs by analyzing the unwritten language, developing an alphabet, and teaching people to read it. Bible translation is moving that whole ladder so that people can get into an attic they very much do want to visit.

So why do we translate the Bible into indigenous languages and teach the people to read their own language? There are many reasons. Here are a few:

- It is not easy to train a college-educated team in linguistics, Bible translation principles, and literacy development, surround them with a group of Ph.D. consultants in every area of expertise needed, and set them to work. In ten or twenty years, they will have produced a society that is growing increasingly literate, and that is reading a Bible in which God speaks their own language.
- The only thing more difficult than this process is setting up a system to teach tens of thousands of illiterate indigenous people to learn to speak and read a language they have no interest in or reason for learning. In comparison, translating the Bible is easier.
- Christianity is based on translation. The first translators were Matthew, Mark, Luke, and John, who translated into Greek the stories that were being repeated in Aramaic, the language Jesus spoke.
- Christianity thrives on translation. Where the proclamation of the Good News was accompanied by the Scriptures in the language of the people, Christianity has spread, blossomed and born fruit. Where the Scriptures existed only in a foreign language, not in the local language, Christianity flourished briefly, then died out or was corrupted.
- God tends to deal with His people in the context of the culture they live in. When the Bible exists in an indigenous language, it allows the Holy Spirit to interpret the application within the culture.
- There are numerous testimonies of people hearing the

Good News in a foreign language and having the basics of the Good News explained to them resulting in their salvation. It is possible for a large number of people to know enough to turn to God eventually, but there are no stories of large churches that are growing firm and strong in their faith and are reaching out to others while they do not have God's Word in their own language.

- God calls His people to translate His Word. A young West African boy, who now calls himself Peter, was unusually bright and quick to learn. Peter caught the eye of a government official visiting his village who brought him out to the city to be educated. Peter learned the official language, excelled in school and became a valued teacher in the city. Somewhere along the way, he met some Christians and heard the Good News. He became a Christian and avidly studied the Bible. After some time, he heard the voice of God within his own heart, "What about the tens of thousands of people back in your tribe's villages? How are they going to hear about Me?" In response, Peter gave up his tenured position as a teacher and joined a Wycliffe partner organization to train a team to help him translate the Bible for his own people.

- Our language is part of our culture. It is part of who we are as people. Linguists have said, "A person is his language." By that they mean our language is not just another skill like playing the piano or riding a bike. We think in language and words as well as in pictures. We use words to express even our deepest feelings. God, therefore, wants to speak the language of every person in every culture in the world.

That's why we translate.

~~~~~~~~~~

The Easter Confusion

I was sitting on the hard-packed red clay of the village central plaza, as I usually did in the late afternoon. From a respectful distance, I strained to hear what the Canela elders' council was saying. I was always hoping to hear a new word or expression to jot down in my little notebook.

"Somebody probably tried to stab him, and he held up his hands. That's how he got holes right through his palms. Yes, I am sure he was killed in a fight."

"No, I heard he was executed. But they didn't club him on the head to kill him, the way we would, they nailed him to a pole and left him to die."

"Yeah, I heard they killed a couple of thieves at the same time."

Suddenly it dawned on me that the village elders were arguing about the death of Jesus. Now I listened even more closely and prayed silently for an opportunity to explain.

Abruptly the chief held up his hand, stopping the argument. "Wait," he said. He pointed at me with his lips and said, "There's our nephew Prejaka. He has been among the Brazilians in town. He probably knows why they treat this week so special."

They called me, and moments later I sat down among the elders. As they crowded closer, I said, "When, long ago, God was on earth, His name was Jesus. He had 12 followers who later wrote down the things He said and did and what happened to Him in the end."

The chief interrupted, "Wouldn't it be good if we had those notebooks! We could just read about it for ourselves."

The elders shook their heads. "But that was long ago, and those notebooks are all lost and gone. Besides, they would be in some language we don't understand."

I breathed a prayer of thanks and said, "Actually, those books did not get lost. They are called the Bible, and they exist in many languages. Remember what I told you before? I am here to translate those books into the Canela language. Last week Jaco and I translated the whole story about the death of Jesus."

The Chief's Command

The chief and the rest of the elders looked shocked. "So why were you just sitting there listening to us old men guessing at what might have happened? Quick! Run! Get those papers and read them to us. We want to know the facts."

A few minutes later, I was back. I handed out some carbon copies of the Passion and Easter story, even though at that time none of them could read. I showed them how to operate the cassette tape player on which I had recorded the translation. The rest of the evening and throughout the next day that cassette player went from the elders' group to the next younger age group, right through to the young initiates. They passed it from house to house until the batteries went dead.

This was the first time the Holy Spirit spoke Canela—the first time the whole village heard a major portion of God's Word in their own language. Although it would still be years before large numbers of Canelas would turn to follow God, this was a great start.

The Confusion Continues

What bothers me is that today, 40 years later, millions of people speaking more than 1600 languages are still just as confused and ignorant about Easter as those Canela elders were.

How much longer will they need to wait to hear that Jesus died and rose again for them?

And hear it in their own language?

~~~~~~~~~~~

What Do the Poor Really Need?

Poor people. You can find them in every country on the globe, regardless of the nation's overall wealth. In North America, we do not see crowds of beggars so typical of India's large cities, but here too, every major city has homeless people and others who live in abject poverty. Television news reports show desperately poor people already destitute, who are suddenly thrown into even more dreadful need, because of hurricanes and earthquakes.

What do poor people need? They beg for money, food, clothing, medical help, and for shelter. Obviously, they need these things urgently, and as followers of Jesus, we have the opportunity and the responsibility to provide these things as acts of love and obedience. In a sense, we see Christ in the faces of the poor. Yet, are these material provisions all that they truly need?

The Real Need of the Poor

Jesus, our master, rabbi, and leader always met the needs of people. Not merely their immediate physical needs, but their deeper and eternal needs. Here is an example from the Master's life. Both Matthew (11:5) and Luke (7:20) tell the story. Some people come to Jesus to find out whether He is the promised Messiah or not. Jesus tells them to look at what He is doing to meet people's needs and on that basis make up their minds.

"The blind see," He points out, "the lame walk, the lepers are cleansed, the deaf hear, the dead raised," and concludes the list by saying "and the poor are given money."

No, not so! That is *not* what He said.

Instead, He focused on the most critical need of the poor and said, "And the poor are being told the Good News."

The Good News? The Gospel? Yes! The good news that God has started to build His kingdom on Earth. The good news that He saves people from the consequences and power of sin. The good news that He transforms them into new creatures. The good news that He directs them to live an utterly different, God-oriented lifestyle—one that tends to lead to food on their table, clothes on their backs, homes to live in, and health for their spirits, minds, and bodies.

Atheist Claims Africa Needs God

Even non-Christians can see the transforming power of this Good News. On December 27, 2008, Matthew Parris, a self-

11

confessed atheist, wrote an article in the *London Sunday Times* called *Africa Needs God*. He agrees with Jesus that what the poor need most is not money, not development assistance, but rather a new worldview. One in which they recognize that God created them as people with the power to change their circumstances—not simply passive, helpless victims of fate with a "whatever will be will be" attitude.

Parris mentioned the development work done by secular non-government organizations, government projects and international aid efforts. He wrote, "These alone will *not* do. Education and training alone will *not* do. In Africa, Christianity changes people's hearts. It brings a spiritual transformation. The rebirth is real. The change is good."

Of course, the change is good! The Good News was designed by God to meet the needs of the people that He created in the same way that specific and powerful antibiotics are designed to kill specific bacteria. People are spiritually, emotionally and physically sick; their lives are messed up in all sorts of ways, but their Designer knows just what they need to heal their sin-infected lives.

God is Not a Note in the Margin

Not every non-Christian can see the power of the Good News as clearly as Parris. People with a worldview that excludes God tend to relegate His Good News to a small corner of life—a little spot kept for religion and isolated from any important area of society. Secularists want to sideline God and His rescue plan for humanity to life's margins, keeping Him out of commerce, education, government, family, or any other area where real life happens. Religion to them is a private, personal matter, or belongs solely in church, a specific building, during set times on Sunday.

That is totally and completely contrary to God's plan. God and His Good News are relevant for every single area of human life. Jesus said, "I am the bread of life" John 6:35 (KJV). Or put another way, "I am to your total life what food is to your physical life." He stands in the spotlight on centre stage, not huddled in some dim corner of an upper balcony. God is the headline, not a note scrawled in the margin.

In the same way that He transforms individuals, families, and villages in Africa, so He transforms people and societies everywhere in the world. Jesus said, "I came that you might have life and that you might have it more abundantly" John 10:10 (KJV). God designed the Good News to fit people for living life—for legislators governing the nation, for teachers mentoring the nation's children, and for business people serving society. All people on earth need God's transforming power working in their lives.

We know that even today, billions of people have yet to hear the Good News. Millions of them speaking more than 1600 languages still have no part of the Good News translated into the language they know best.

That is why the last thing Jesus did on Earth was to commission His followers to go out into every part of the world and tell everyone this Good News and how they too, can be transformed.

That is why we—His followers today, who have heard God's Good News and were transformed by its power, put Jesus on centre stage, and make Him the headline.

That is why we spare no expense but commit our lives to do whatever it takes to tell the Good News to the poor everywhere on earth.

Or do we?

~~~~~~~~~~

Grandson Sees Impact of God's Word in Jamaican

When he was 21 years old our grandson, Tyler Vanderveen, worked for eight months with Wycliffe Caribbean in Jamaica as part of the on-site internship with his school, Ambrose University, and the Christian and Missionary Alliance denomination in Canada. Tyler worked under director John

Roomes whom Jo and I recruited, oriented, and trained when I was director of Wycliffe Caribbean in the early 2000s.

Tyler experienced, first hand, the power of the translated Word to draw people to Christ. Here's Tyler's Report in his own words:

While returning with my boss John Roomes from a Wycliffe retreat we passed through the town of Kendall, about 70 kilometres east of Kingston. We stopped to participate in a *March for Righteousness* gathering in the town square at which John's brother had asked him to speak. Two local pastors had already preached to the group gathered before the stage, reading the gospel of Luke from the New King James version.

Not English but Jamaican

John, however, did not speak in English as the pastors had but spoke in Jamaican Patois. He also focused his preaching, not at the group of Christians near the stage but at the group of men playing dominoes across the street, at the taxi drivers in the parking lot, and at the people in the market.

Soon a small crowd gathered at the edge of the market, listening intently. In the first minute that John began to read from the gospel of Luke, recently translated into Jamaican, a homeless man ran all the way from the back right to the stage, his face alight with understanding. At the same time, some Rastafarian men who were listening to the event from behind some trees came around to the front to listen.

I had already been told that many people in the rural parts of Jamaica do not understand English well. I had taken that to mean the people in the hills and far from the cities. But, on the way back to Kingston, John told me unless a person lives in one of the two main cities, Kingston or Montego Bay, they probably don't understand English that well. The business people or those who finished high school will speak it better but the poorer, less educated people won't.

Hope for Rastafarians

John also told me that the Rastafarian religion split off from orthodox Christianity because they wanted to maintain a sense of their African heritage by emphasizing a more central role for Ethiopia in Bible history and theology. They wanted a Bible in Jamaican Patois that they could understand. Most of what they believe is loosely based on a version of the Bible that they can't really understand.

It seems that every time the church in Jamaica moves toward being more Jamaican and less British, Rastafarians are interested. They are watching and waiting for a church which accepts them.

John says that when the whole Bible is finally translated into Jamaican and churches begin to preach from it; many Rastafarian people will come to the Lord. They have tried to understand but could not in the English speaking churches. But now, when they hear the Bible taught in their own Jamaican Patois language, all the truths they gleaned from the old English Bible will be strengthened and the things they got wrong will become obvious and will be corrected.

Prayer for Revival in Jamaica

This is an exciting time to be working in Jamaica. First, God is beginning to use the portions of the Bible that are already translated into Jamaican to draw many people to Himself. Also, during this 50th year of Jamaican independence churches all across Jamaica are praying and working for revival and renewal. Pastors compare the ever-present crime, corruption, violence, drugs, and gangs as chains that must be thrown off before Jamaica can flourish. These Satanic bonds can only be broken through the power of God's Word in the language of the people.

Many pastors and church groups are praying that God will make this 50th anniversary a year of Jubilee as it was in the Old Testament. We are praying that the bonds of crime and violence in Jamaica will be thrown off. We are praying for revival. All the things that are holding Jamaica away from God will be removed, as the bonds of the self-enslaved man would be removed in the year of jubilee.

Please join in prayer for Jamaica. Pray that the love and power of Jesus will restore Jamaica, that revival and renewal would come to Jamaica.

~~~~~~~~~~

Correcting the United Nations

Many a bet has been settled in beer bars and liquor lounges by referring to the Guinness Book of World Records. (No, I'm not drawing on personal experience—I saw it on TV!) Since the Guinness book is so valuable for resolving arguments, you'd assume that its researchers would follow the ancient wisdom of the journalism adage, "When gathering facts, make sure they are."

Turns out that would be an unwarranted assumption.

Take, for instance, the area of translation. Here is what I read on the United Nations website of the Office of the High Commissioner for Human Rights (2006). "The Office of the High Commissioner for Human Rights has been awarded the Guinness World Record for having collected, translated and disseminated the Universal Declaration of Human Rights into more than 300 languages and dialects: from Abkhaz to Zulu. The Universal Declaration is thus the document most translated—indeed, the most 'universal'—in the world."

What? Only 300 languages? And Guinness accepted that as a world record?

Let's see. When the UN was founded in 1945, a Bible, a New Testament or some substantial amount of Scripture had already been translated into about 1,000 languages. Including the preamble, the 30 articles of the Universal Declaration have 1,773 words in English. That's nearly the same length as Jesus' speech on how people should relate to God and each other, in Matthew 5 and 6, or about two and a half pages of the 750-page

Canela partial Bible, which my wife and I translated.

In comparison, during the past 58 years, this very brief UN document was translated into 321 languages. During the same 58 years, full Bibles, New Testaments, or whole books were translated into 1,700 languages.

Letter to the United Nations

This discrepancy stirred me up, so I wrote to Mary Robinson, the UN High Commissioner for Human Rights:

Date: April 29, 2006
Subject: UDHR most translated document? Not quite.
High Commissioner for Human Rights

Dear Ms. Robinson,

You have a right to be pleased and excited to see the UDHR being translated into so many of the world's languages and dialects. Your enthusiasm, however, may have gotten the best of your office when it published these paragraphs on your website.

The UDHR being translated into 300 languages is impressive, but the full Bible has been translated into 422 languages, and the full New Testament of the Bible into a further 1,079 languages. 876 other languages have at least one book of the Bible translated into them. That totals 2,377 languages that have at least some major portion of the Bible translated into them. Besides that, a further 1,640 languages have Bible translation projects going on in them right now.

What interests me, as a Bible translator for the Ramkokamekra-Canela people of northeast Brazil, is that the concepts and principles of the Universal Declaration of Human Rights are found in, and based on, the rights stated so clearly in the Bible. So, in a way, we Bible translators are doing our part in helping to lay a foundation for your excellent work around the world.

Sincerely,
Jack D. Popjes

A substantial portion of the Bible will be translated and disseminated into every one of the world's 6,900-plus languages long before the United Nations' Universal Declaration of Human Rights manages the same feat.

The Guinness Book of World Records notwithstanding, you won't go wrong to bet on that.

By the way, I never received any acknowledgment from Ms. Robinson, but I did notice that the Guinness World Records webpage stating the UN claim has been removed.

~~~~~~~~~~~

Contempt for a Holy Book

Each day, as my family and I visited the little one-room house with the hole in the seat, we used a page of an old Eaton's catalogue instead of toilet paper. This showed no disrespect for the Eaton's company or for its products; it was just common money-saving practice in rural Canada during the 1950s.

I remembered those years while reading newspaper accounts of military prison guards being accused of tearing pages out of Islam's holy book, the Quran, and flushing them down the toilet.

Disrespecting the Quran was a highly effective way of showing contempt for Muslim prisoners and their religion.

The Quran

The Quran is the focal point of all Islam. It is held as the uncreated word of God, written on golden tablets in Paradise. For Muslims today, the Quran is both a physical proof for Islam, and its reading is the sound of Islam. Reciting the Quran in Arabic creates a sacred and spiritually powerful moment. Muslims believe the Quran can never be correctly translated into any other language because Arabic was made a holy language when Allah used it for his final revelation to humanity. They also believe that the Quran uniquely records the actual spoken words of Allah as opposed to the Judeo-Christian idea of a divinely inspired and universal message that can be expressed in many other languages.

True believers read the Quran aloud in Arabic. No wonder, therefore, Muslims around the world were appalled and infuriated when stories of such a gross desecration of the Quran began to spread.

Although we, as Christians, believe the Bible to be the Word of God, we do not consider the Hebrew and Greek languages in which it was written to be holy. In contrast to Islam, Christianity is a religion that depends on translation of the Bible. No true believer needs to learn Hebrew, Greek or even Latin to recite the Bible and create a holy moment. Instead, God's Holy Spirit speaks through the translated Scriptures, revealing God to the hearts of people. What's more, only where the Bible has been translated into the heart language of the people has Christianity flourished.

The Bible

Although Christians do not consider a copy of the Bible to be holy in the same way that Muslims consider the Quran holy, we do respect the physical book. I recently realized this anew during an intensive inspection of my carry-on luggage at an airport in the U.S.

The white-gloved inspector repacked my case, placing my Sunday shoes on top of my brown leather Bible. As I reached in to change the arrangement, he angrily told me to keep my hands out of my case.

So I asked him to move the Bible, wrap it in a T-shirt, and put it in last, on top of all the contents. He did so, giving me a look that said, "Weirdo religious fundamentalist fanatic!"

Some people have no problem with putting their shoes on top of their Bible. I can't even put my Bible on the floor. Maybe that is going overboard. Never mind. What bothers me more is the disrespect many Christians show the Bible by going day after day without reading it. We may read it as a habit, or as liturgy, but in so doing our minds and hearts are disconnected from one another. That is major disrespect.

Others read it and even think about it, but do not obey it. That is like reading a love letter wherein they ask you to do something, and then ignoring it. That is neither an act of love nor of respect.

Disrespect for the Bible

Individual Christians are not the only ones who disrespect God's Word. The Church, as a whole, does too. Now, 2,000 years after the Bible was written, over a quarter of the world's languages still have no translation of even a single verse of God's Word. Although the Church around the world has benefited from having the Scriptures in the heart languages of the people in its pews, it still has not passed God's Word on to everyone. There are still 114 million people speaking 1636 languages, in continents such as Africa and Asia, in which not one verse of the Bible has yet been translated. That is the greatest disrespect.

No Christian would dream of using a page of the Bible as toilet paper. Yet statistics show that the Church as a whole still struggles to set Bible translation as a high priority.

That, too, is holding the sacred Word of God in contempt.

~~~~~~~~~~

A Long History of Criticism of Bible Translation

Jamaican Patois versus English

While the nations gathered in Beijing to battle it out in the Olympic sports arenas, a different battle, but also with ancient traditions, raged in Jamaica. The September 2008 issue of *Christianity Today* magazine reported on the controversy. It surrounded the ongoing translation of the Bible into Jamaican Creole, also called *patois*, which is the language spoken fluently by the vast majority of the population. While English is the official language of Jamaica, most children grow up speaking *patois/patwa* and learn English in school. Authorities do not think of it as a real language, and, therefore, the word *"patois"* is not written with a capital letter.

Letters to the newspaper editors and callers to radio phone-in programs pushed forward the usual objections to translating the Bible into *patois*—the language spoken by about two million Jamaicans: "The common language is not good enough to express the concepts of the Bible." They also urged the usual advice, "Speakers of *patois* just need to learn English better."

Common Latin versus Classical Latin, Greek, and Hebrew

It seems that for centuries, whenever the Bible was translated, the new translation was criticised. Jerome translated the Bible into Latin around 400 AD. It was criticised because he had not translated it into the classical Latin used by orators and poets, but into the common, everyday Latin spoken by people on the street and at home. That is why Jerome's translation was called the Vulgate. It was vulgar, not in the sense of being indecent, but of being common.

Canela versus Portuguese

Disapproval of new translations is routine. Even the partial Bible that my wife and I translated—with the help of gifted and trained Canela associates was disparaged. Imagine that!

Whenever I showed the Canela Bible to Portuguese speaking Brazilian pastors, they automatically assumed that the translation in Canela was not as clear, as accurate, or as good as the Bible they used in preaching to their Portuguese speaking congregations.

I did not argue with them, but I knew from sitting in their church services that they read the archaic three-hundred-year-old Portuguese Ferreira de Almeida version, then took most of the sermon time to explain to the congregation what the passage meant before making an application. I could have told them that no one needed to explain what the Bible in Canela says—it speaks clearly right off the page.

Plautdietsch versus German

Wherever in the world the Bible is translated into minority languages, someone will probably level criticism at it. When the Bible was translated into Plautdietsch, or Low German, the translation was criticised for not being in a language worthy to hold God's Word. People who speak fluent German do not consider Plautdietsch as a real language, just bad German. That's not true, of course. It is a legitimate language spoken by hundreds of thousands of Mennonite people as their native language.

Even today, church leaders in some Mennonite groups still insist on reading only the German Bible in church services, even though most of the hearers don't understand German well. The rest of the service, including the preaching and praying, is in Plautdietsch.

English versus Latin

In having their work scorned, the translators of the Bible into Jamaican *patois*, as well as the translation teams currently working in nearly two thousand other minority languages around the world, are in good company.

John Wycliffe was criticized strongly for translating the Bible into English, the first major translation since Jerome's Vulgate a thousand years earlier. A contemporary historian and fellow clergyman, Henry Knighton spoke for the clergy of his day when he criticised the first translation into English under the following points:

"Christ gave the Scriptures to the clergy and doctors of the Church so that they could use it to meet the needs of lay people and other weaker (uneducated) persons. John Wycliffe has now translated it into common English which has laid the Bible more open to literate laymen and women than it has formerly been to the most learned of the clergy. The jewel of the Church, hitherto the principal gift of the clergy and the divines, has now been cast abroad, and trodden under foot of swine, and is now made ever more common to laypeople."

Henry Knighton used the wrong metaphor. The Word of God is not a jewel to be preserved in a glass case, admired, and taught by the well-educated chosen few. Jesus Himself called God's Word seed meant to be scattered generously everywhere and to sprout in prepared soil.

In the same way, the Creator made men and women in His own image, with the capacity to hear Him and communicate with Him. The Word of God can give receptive people the power to change their lives, deepen their understanding of God, and grow in love for Him.

But they must hear the Word of God first—in the language they understand best!

~~~~~~~~~~

Language Change and Bible Translation

The whole issue of languages—nearly 7,000 of them currently spoken around the world—is bewildering. It is meant to be. Perplexity was the original plan. God confused the languages of humanity at the tower of Babel—as the babble started, the building stopped. (Genesis 11:1-9)

Our God loves variety. The diversity of His creation, plants, animals, and people overwhelms us. He not only created people in numerous races, but he also gave us distinct personalities, making each one of us unique and different from every other human being. No wonder, then, that when He created languages, He created the potential for ongoing and growing variety.

Some people think language is like a finely polished precious stone, to be kept clean and unchanged. What utter nonsense! The world's languages are living things, constantly changing and growing like plants and bushes and trees. The more a language is used, the more it is likely to change and grow.

That is why English, for example, has grown and changed so much in the past few hundred years. The language Shakespeare used in his poetry and plays, and in which the

King James Authorized Version of the Bible was translated, sounds strange to modern ears. It is beautiful in its own right, and well worth studying, but it is no longer the language we speak at work, in school and with our friends and family.

Language Trees

The world's languages are like a grove of several dozen trees, each as different from each other as poplar, palm, pear, and pine trees. Just as each tree has a trunk, major limbs, branches and leafy twigs, so the twigs and branches of linguistic trees are related to each other while being utterly unrelated to twigs on the other trees.

This sounds simple, but it isn't. Twigs from different trees don't change when they rub against each other, but languages do. When speakers of one language come into close contact with people speaking other languages, the rate at which languages change and grow increases.

My colleague Hart Wiens served for years as the chairman of the Wycliffe Canada board and is the Director of Scripture Translations for the Canadian Bible Society. He illustrated this aspect of change and growth when he commented on the languages spoken by the Mennonites and Amish. Hart gives some fascinating history showing how these languages developed:

"One language is Plautdietsch spoken by Russian Mennonites. This is essentially Low Saxon that was spoken in Holland and taken by Mennonite emigrants to Prussia and then Russia where it developed further. This language is not understood at all by the Amish, who speak a language which they call Pennsylvania Deitsch. Outsiders mistakenly call it Pennsylvania Dutch. It is far from Dutch. It is more closely related to the German dialects spoken in Bavaria and Switzerland where the ancestors of this group of Mennonites fled to escape persecution. Later they immigrated to Pennsylvania and then to other states, as well as Waterloo County in Ontario."

What is a Real Language?

Another misunderstanding about common non-prestige languages like Jamaican Patois is that since they are not written they are not *real* languages. More nonsense! Language is what comes out of people's mouths! Language is not the writing system. Scores of writing systems exist around the world, but they are not what makes a language different.

In Asia, for example, the Bible was translated into a language spoken by a people group who lived in four different adjacent countries. Each of these countries used a completely different writing system. At an international Christian conference, some speakers of that language came from all four countries, looked at each other's Bibles printed in such diverse symbols, and shook their heads in confusion. Then they stood side by side and read a passage from Psalm 119 aloud from their own Bibles—in complete unison using the same spoken words.

The Growth of Creole Languages

Sometimes a branch of a healthy bush dies, the leaves withering and falling off, while another part of the same bush flourishes and sprouts new leaves. In the same way, some languages die off and become extinct while other languages develop. Many of the world's newer languages are a form of Creole in which the new, developing language borrows words from other languages, but has its own unique grammatical system. With or without a writing system, they are real languages.

Often a Creole language is spoken in a country where a prestige language like English, French or Spanish is the official language. Invariably speakers of the Creole language are pressured to stop speaking that "bad English" (or bad French or bad Spanish) and speak "proper English." This is the case in Jamaica where the official language is English, and the majority language is Jamaican Patois.

My colleague Dr. Jo-Anne Ferreira is a lecturer in linguistics at The University of the West Indies, St. Augustine. She commented, "If Patois or Patwa is not capitalized (as for English and French), and if it is written 'patois,' then people will continue to ignore it as a real and proper language. The better name for the language is Jamaican, not Patois, Patwa or Jamaican Creole."

Ignorance and Cultural Bias by Leaders

Governmental or educational authorities often do not understand the nature of language, and some may suffer from cultural bias. They tend to look down on non-prestige languages and consider them a hindrance to education and economic development. There is a long, sad, and unproductive history of government policies forbidding children to speak their native language and forcing them to learn to read in the official language—often when they could not speak it. That approach simply does not work. Only the very brightest students learn to read well, the vast majority do not.

Bilingual education, starting in the language the student knows best and going from there to the official language has been successful in countries all around the world. People's first language, even if it is an officially despised Creole language, will usually be their heart language, and the language in which they will best understand God's love for them.

~~~~~~~~~~~

Bible Translation Enriches the Worldwide Church

"From countless pulpits every week we hear an implicit message that has wormed its way into our minds: we lack the key to unlocking the secrets of Scripture because we don't know the original languages."

This is the first sentence of an article by Jost Zetzsche in the April 2013 issue of *Christianity Today* titled "Knowing What the Bible *Really* Means" subtitled, *Why Multiple Translations Might Even Be Better Than Scripture In Its Original Languages.*

The author draws a parallel with pre-Reformation times when

illiterate churchgoers had to depend on church authorities to tell them what the Bible said and meant.

God's View of Languages

God, Who invented languages and implanted them in people way back at the Tower of Babel, loves languages. All languages. There is no special holy Bible language—not Hebrew, not Greek, not Aramaic, not even Latin or Shakespearian English. God reveals Himself in His Word, and He wants it translated into all the world's languages so everyone may know His great love for people.

Every time the Word of God is translated into a new language, the process brings new meanings to the surface and reveals insights into the depths of God's Word. Thus, Bible translation is capable of bringing a deeper level of understanding to readers all over the world, as well as adding to our collective knowledge about the truths that God is eager for us to find.

A Real-Life Illustration

I remember how this happened when we were translating Luke 7 into Canela. It's the story of local Jewish leaders who came to Jesus asking Him to heal the servant of a Roman centurion, saying, "This man deserves to have you do this because he loves our nation and has built our synagogue."

For each of the English first person plural pronouns ("we," "us" and "our"), the Canela language has two words, *mepa,* and *mei. Mepa* is used when the person spoken to is included, and *mei*, when the person spoken to, is excluded.

For example, let's say I am teaching a class and say, "We *(mepa)* are studying Luke," meaning "We (including you who are listening to me) are studying Luke." If someone poked his head in the door and asked what we were studying, I would say, "We *(mei)* are studying Luke," meaning, "We (but not you) are studying Luke."

So it was easy to translate, "He loves our *(mepa)* nation." Since

Jesus was part of the Jewish nation, the Jewish leaders included Him. But then came the second part, "He has built our synagogue."

This synagogue was in Capernaum where Jesus lived and where many of His disciples lived. If the Jewish leaders considered Jesus a member of the Capernaum synagogue, they would use the word *mepa*, including Jesus. If, however, they did not consider Him a member of their synagogue, they would use *mei*, excluding Jesus.

Greek Class Dilemma

One day I posed this problem to a group of third-year Greek students in a seminary and joked with them, saying, "Look it up in Greek." Their knowledge of Greek was useless in this case since neither Greek nor English considers the inclusive and exclusive aspects of the person spoken to.

It took some study on the part of the seminarians to come up with a good decision based on the fact that He was known everywhere as "Jesus of Nazareth." The Canelas, however, don't need to study the situation. They can simply read the *mei*, excluding Jesus, in the text we translated and know instantly that the Jewish leaders considered Jesus a member of another synagogue.

The New Testament has many such examples. Try reading 2nd Corinthians 5 and decide when the pronouns "we," "us" and "our" refer to the Corinthian Christians (*mepa*, inclusive) and when they refer only to the writers Paul and Timothy (*mei*, exclusive). We translated the pronouns in verses 1 to 10 as *mepa*, including the Corinthians, but in verse 11 we switched to *mei*, excluding them.

The Canela portion of God's worldwide Church has, in this small area of meaning, a better insight into Scripture than people who read the Bible only in English or Greek. This subtle but significant facet of their language adds an extra layer of insight and meaning to a part of speech that most English speakers would casually overlook.

The Blessing of Bible Translation to the Whole Church

Thousands of languages all over the world have unique features that force translators to explore deeper meanings and gather further insights and thereby bring the readers into a greater understanding of the Word of God.

Long ago, God began to reveal Himself to humanity through the Holy Spirit by inspiring prophets and apostles to write His Word. Ever since then, this same Holy Spirit has been helping scholars to translate it into the 7000 languages of the world, thereby increasingly revealing more of Himself to the world's peoples.

The Church as a whole is, therefore, enriched through Bible translation as it expands our horizons and broadens our knowledge of God's Word.

Section Two: How the Bible is Translated

It's All About Family.

God wants all people to know Him, to become part of His Family.

A Bible translator's main job is, therefore, to translate the Bible so God can introduce Himself to an indigenous people.

And what is God's first job? To prepare the indigenous people to accept the introducer.

Fifty years ago, in the spring of 1968, the Canela people of Brazil took the *second* step in accepting my wife, Jo, and me as part of their native society. They adopted us as members of their families and full citizens of Canela society.

The Canela adoption/initiation ceremony involved lots of red ochre paint, plenty of tree-sap glue and white hawk down all over our bodies. Surrounded by crowds of Canelas, we listened to the chief's long speech; then each of the sub-chiefs and elders made shorter speeches.

We couldn't understand a word.

A month earlier, when I first met the Canela chief in town, the Canelas had taken the *first* step in accepting us. Although he knew only a little Portuguese, he understood that we were ready to live in the village, learn Canela, and help where we could. He pantomimed giving me an injection in my upper arm and made writing motions. "Yes," I said, "we will treat sick people and teach you to read and write."

"You come," he said.

A few days later, I stood in the centre of the Canela village plaza surrounded by a large group of somber, silent, serious looking Canela men. I faced a village elder who, leaning on his spear, chanted loudly for long time.

I couldn't understand a word.

Abruptly he stopped chanting, and shouted, "Prejaka! Prejaka! Prejakaaaa!" at which all those silent men behind me suddenly shouted, "Yuhaaa!"

Major adrenaline rush!

Then they all broke into smiles, grabbed my hands and kept saying "Prejaka, Prejaka, Prejaka." I finally got it! I had just been given a Canela name—the *first* step into being accepted into Canela culture.

Later on Jo, and each of our daughters went through the same naming ceremony. It was a once and for all time event. But over the next few decades, we went through the adoption/re-initiation ceremony dozens of times—each time we returned to the village after an extended time away. And eventually we fully understood all those speeches.

"We have adopted you into our village and into our families. You are even more one of us now than when you first came to us. You now speak our language. You invented a way to write our language and taught us to read and write in it, and to count and read numbers. "

"You are training teachers from among our young people. You help them make books for us. You have saved many lives with your medicine, especially our babies. You are family and belong here."

"Join any festival. Go anywhere in the Canela lands. Take pictures of any of us, and of any of our festivals. When outsiders come in just to look and take pictures, we ask them for gifts, but we will never ask you."

Still true.

Nine years ago, after an absence of nineteen years, we re-visited the village. Yes, once again, glue, feathers, red body paint and a wide-open village welcome to our whole family—fifteen of us—including our eight grandchildren.

God arrived in the Canela village long before we came. He arrived to prepare the villagers, so they would adopt us, and make us citizens of the Canela village. God stayed there with us for twenty-two years. When we left, He didn't leave.

He stayed in the village. He is still there, adopting many Canelas into His Family and accepting them as citizens in His Kingdom.

~~~~~~~~~~

Do Not Despise the Day of Small Beginnings

The Question

Hearing that my wife and I had translated much of the Bible into a Brazilian indigenous language, a man asked me, "What was the first thing you translated?" He was astonished when I answered, "The story of the gingerbread man."

"I can't believe it!" he exclaimed, "You're missionary Bible translators! Why waste time translating a kids' fairy tale?"

The Answer

I explained to him that we were just learning to translate and that this story, with its small vocabulary and a large amount of repetition, was easier to translate than a Scripture passage. "Even so, I expect to make mistakes," I added, "and I'd rather make errors in a children's story than in a Scripture passage."

Translating children's fairy stories was the small beginning that two decades later led to an accurately translated 750-page Bible, with 250 pages of Old Testament and 500 pages of New Testament. When we returned to Canada, every Canela home had a Bible, and at least one person in each home could read it, having learned to read using the orthography and educational materials we had developed. The Church continues to grow from the seed of the Word, and many Canelas now live without fear of evil spirits.

The Lesson

Although that children's story was a tiny beginning, we learned and practiced some enduring translation principles. I also learned the truth of the adage, "Something is Better than Nothing." The Bible is replete with examples of this fact. Jesus solved the problem of feeding five-thousand men and their families by starting with one boy's lunch of five small loaves and two small fish. It wasn't much, but He started with something. (John 6.)

The prophet Elisha started with a tiny flask of olive oil, but this oil expanded miraculously to fill every available container in the neighbourhood. There was so much olive oil, it not only paid off a huge debt, there was enough left to buy food for three people throughout an extended time of famine. (2 Kings 4: 1-7)

God's Question

When Almighty God appeared to Moses and told him he would lead the Israelites out of Egypt, Moses was filled with doubt. So God asked him "What is that in your hand?"

"A staff," Moses replied. (Exodus 4:1-3). That simple wooden walking stick was the small Something that impressed Pharaoh by turning into a snake, then brought plagues on Egypt, split the waters of the Red Sea, brought water out of a rock, and was the focal point of prayer that gave victory in battle.

My wife and I faced a gigantic Bible translation task. Where do we start? It was as if God said, "What is that in your hand?" A children's story. It was something, and we learned to translate by starting with that story.

What About You?

Any of us, facing a massive project or a messy problem, needs to turn to God for help. Don't be surprised if He asks, "What is that in your hand?"

Then look, see what you have to make a start, a small beginning. Then do it. Make that start. Begin with what is in your hand, and trust God to step in to do His Miracle of Expansion. A half cup of olive oil into barrels full. A boy's lunch into a feast

33

for thousands. An ordinary hiking stick imbued with miracle-working power.

What is that in your hand? Something small, relatively insignificant? Doesn't matter. Use it to make a small beginning and trust God to expand it to meet needs, solve problems, and erase doubts.

"Do not despise these small beginnings, for the Lord rejoices to see the work begin." (Zechariah 4:10 NLT)

~~~~~~~~~~~

The Curious Case of the Constipated Church

Christianity is unique! It is the only major world religion that did *not* preserve the words of its Founder in the language in which He spoke them. Aramaic was the language commonly spoken in Palestine during Jesus life. Jesus spoke hundreds of thousands of words during His three years of public ministry, but only a dozen words are preserved in Aramaic. Matthew, Mark, Luke, and John took all of the Aramaic oral records of His teachings, conversations, and prayers, and translated them into Greek—a completely different language totally unrelated to Aramaic.

Christianity Depends on Bible Translation

Ever since then, Christianity has depended on translation to enter thousands of cultures and languages in every nation of the world. Bible translation is, therefore, basic and foundational to the growth and health of Christianity. As a Bible translator, it disturbs me that this critical fact is not taught in Sunday schools or mentioned from the pulpit. It would stop much misunderstanding and controversy about Bible translation.

Ignoring Culture Creates Misunderstanding

No one disputes the need to translate God's Word into the *language* of the target readers and audience. The disagreement comes when godly, well-meaning people, who honour the Word of God, insist on ignoring the *culture* of the target audience.

Most of these critics do not understand what it means to translate from one culture into another culture. Metaphors, for instance, often vary widely among cultures. The translators of the 1611 *King James Authorized Version*, for example, tended to be quite literal, translating the metaphors common in Greek culture into English word for word, without regard to how their translation would be interpreted by people who knew only English culture.

Think of Paul's concern about the Corinthian church people being constipated. Constipated? Well, that is what it sounds like to English ears, especially today. "Ye are not straitened in us, but ye are straitened in your own bowels" (2 Cor. 6:12, KJV). Most of us know that "strait" means "narrow" or "constricted," and "constricted bowels" is a good description of constipation. But that is far from what Paul meant!

Greek culture considered the *bowels* to be the seat of emotion. English culture, on the other hand, thinks of the *heart* as the place of feelings and affections. The Canelas talk of the *ear*, other cultures of the *liver* or the *throat*, etc. Weymouth's version goes half way when he translates, "There is no narrowness in our love to you, the narrowness is in your own feelings" (WNT). "Narrowness" still sounds unnatural to us, but at least he abandoned the "bowels" and uses "love" and "feelings." Using our English culture's metaphor, we could translate it, "Our hearts are open to you, but yours are closed to us." Without the metaphor, it is simply, "We love you, but you don't love us."

Translating Metaphors to Fit Canela Culture

When Jo and I translated Matthew 24:41 into Canela, we had a similar problem. Jesus foretells the end times, "Two women shall be grinding at the mill; the one shall be taken, and the other left." The mill used at that time was made of two flat, round stones.

Our problem was that the Canelas do not grind grain, and the local stones are chunks of lava rock—useless for grinding. We had to discard the "grinding" metaphor. Wanting a clear, dynamic translation, we asked ourselves, "What is there in the Canela culture that would give a similar picture, and that would carry the same meaning as the original?"

Every morning during rice harvest, pairs of women pound rice to separate the kernels from the hulls. The rice is in a large mortar—a hollowed hardwood log standing on end. The pestles are metre-long clubs. We used to wake up every morning to their rhythmic THUNK—thonk, THUNK—thonk. If one woman disappeared, no one would even need to look since the single THUNK—...., THUNK—.... sound alone would carry the message.

The First Translators: Our Examples

"But you are changing the Word of God!" some folk have told me. Yes, in a way I am. But I am in good company. The first translators, Matthew, Mark, Luke, and John, also chose different words as they focused not only on the language but also on the culture, which is the way of life of their readers and therefore their way of understanding the world. Matthew wrote his Gospel keeping Jewish culture in mind, while Luke and Mark wrote for people in the Greco-Roman culture.

Dr. Wayne Dye* is an International Consultant for Scripture Use in SIL—Wycliffe's field partner. He points out the startling differences. In two parallel passages describing the same scene—Matthew 16:13 and Mark 8:27—Matthew translates Jesus as saying, "Whom do men say that I the *Son of Man* am?" while Mark simply translates, "Whom do men say that I am?" (KJV).

Did Mark leave out something that Jesus said? Yes, he did! He left out an obscure third person term that Matthew's Jewish readers would know referred to the Messiah. But Mark was willing, under the guidance of God's Holy Spirit, to leave out that ambiguous meaning to make sure he did not confuse his non-Jewish readers.

36

Jesus said, "Kingdom of Heaven" They Wrote, "Kingdom of God."

Even more startling is how Mark, and Luke each changed what Jesus actually said in Aramaic to fit the cultural understanding of their Greco-Roman audiences. Dr. Dye writes, "In many passages, Matthew reported Jesus as talking about the *Kingdom of Heaven*. In every parallel passage, Mark and Luke translated this as *Kingdom of God*. Mark and Luke never use the phrase *Kingdom of Heaven*.

The cultural difference explains it. Matthew's Jewish readers would understand *Heaven* to mean the place where God reigns. Mark and Luke's Greek readers would have thought of the *Kingdom of Heaven* as the home of their Greek pantheon, a rather tacky group of gods and goddesses—a concept totally different from Jesus' original meaning."

To make the biblical message clear, modern translators must follow the example of the first translators and keep in mind their readers' language, cultures and world-views.

Matthew, Mark, and Luke chose terms to fit not only the *language* spoken by their readers, but also the *culture* of their respective audiences to produce a dynamic, culture-sensitive, meaning-based translation.

Bible translators for all the world's nearly seven thousand languages and cultures today need to follow the biblical examples set by these first translators. To translate into the readers' *language* but ignore their *culture* spreads needless confusion and misunderstanding.

*(Private correspondence in 2007 with Dr. T. Wayne Dye about his book, *The Bible Translation Strategy* (Dallas: Wycliffe Bible Translators, 1980)

~~~~~~~~~~

"Whoops! There's no word for it."

Those of you who are fluent in more than one language have

no doubt experienced this when you translate from one language and culture into another. The more different the languages and cultures, the more often it happens.

As a Bible translator for the Canela people in Brazil, I constantly ran into this problem. Jesus taught, "Unless a grain of wheat falls into the ground and dies, it remains alone; but if it dies, it produces much grain." John 12:24.

Since wheat is unknown among the Canela, their language had no word for it. This was an easy one to solve. We simply substituted "wheat" with "rice" since a grain of rice in the shell looks and acts the same as a grain of wheat. It was a simple case of using "cultural equivalence instead of lexical equivalence" which is linguist-speak for "if there is no word for the thing, find something like it in the culture."

It sounds easy. Sometimes it is, but usually not.

Long ago an explorer traveled to the icy shores of the Canadian north. He may have been a Christian because he left behind a translation of the Shepherd's Psalm (23) in the local indigenous language. Unfortunately, he had depended on an interpreter to translate for him. The indigenous people memorized the lines and passed them on to their children.

A generation or two later a missionary linguist/translator arrived, settled among these people, and learned the language. When, after some years, he began to translate the Bible, his indigenous language helper told him, "We already have some of God's Book," and to prove it recited some verses of the well known and much loved Psalm 23.

The missionary was aghast. Obviously, the interpreter had tried to use some cultural equivalents but with disastrous results. Here are the first two verses, with some explanations:

v.1 The Lord is my shepherd, I shall not want

The interpreter substituted "sheep" with "wild mountain goats." The closest translation for "herding" was "doing something with animals" which in the case of wild goats was to hunt them.

The word "my" carried the meaning "one who works for me."

The first verse of the Psalm went like this:

God is my goat hunter,

I don't want him!

The second verse didn't fare much better.

v.2 He makes me lie down in green pastures,

The part "he makes me" was interpreted as "he forces me to do something against my will." The only green is found on the sun-facing-sides of mountains.

He leads me beside still waters.

"To lead" is to pull an animal along by a rope around the neck. The only "still water" is the sea.

The first two verses therefore went:

God is my goat hunter,

I don't want him!

For He flings me down on the mountainside,

and drags me down to the sea.

How do translators avoid this kind of disaster?

Obviously, they need to understand the meaning of the passage. They also need to know the language and culture. But beyond those two basics, translators need to know the translation principles to obey and the techniques to use. This requires intensive training and continuing study.

That's why I am glad a wealth of how-to-translate-the-Bible material is being made available to indigenous translators via computer-based training programs. Hundreds of trained Christian men and women are now engaged in translating God's Word into their own languages, using proven techniques and principles of Bible translation.

Without this training the translator risks turning God, our loving Shepherd, into an abusive goat hunter who well deserves to be fired.

~~~~~~~~~~

To Focus on the Message, Eliminate Distraction

No distractions! Eliminate anything in your presentation that might distract your audience from the point of your talk.

Public speaker coaches hammer this advice repeatedly. Don't tempt your hearers with distractions. Don't wear an outfit that calls attention to itself. No flamboyant ties. No unusual outfits. If a story doesn't relate to your point, delete it, no matter how good it is. It will sidetrack some of your listeners.

Public speakers, pastors, and teachers all know reducing distraction is a basic principle of communication.

The same is true for pioneer missionaries working in an indigenous village. Jo and I had a vitally important message to communicate while living among the Canela for over twenty years.

"Your Creator God loves you and wants you to know and love Him. He sent His Son to save you. God will fill you with His Spirit so you can relate to others in peace and love. He will fill you with peace and power so that you no longer fear death and evil spirits."

We modeled this message for the Canela—living in peace with them, loving them, and living without fear, totally trusting God's care for us no matter what happened.

But we knew we had some built-in distractions. I was tall, blonde, and blue-eyed. We were foreign, speaking English to our kids and to each other. We were rich. Jo had, not one pan, but two, as well as a kettle; we seemed to have an unlimited supply of matches, and plenty of salt. We had more than one pair of shorts or piece of cloth each. I wore a watch, the only one in the village. Instead of eating with our hands from a cast iron pan on the clay floor, we ate with spoons from enamel plates at a table.

We were concerned that our foreignness and wealth would

blind the Canelas so that they could not see that the peace and love they saw in us, came from our relationship with the Creator God.

Jo and I reduced this distraction by living as much as possible like the Canelas around us. We lived in a house with a clay floor, dried-mud walls and a palm-thatch roof, just like our neighbours. We ate what they ate, we learned their language, learned their songs, participated in their festivals and practiced generosity and became Canelas as much as we could.

We could afford a propane stove and refrigerator, which would have saved us much time, work, and inconvenience, but did without them for those decades. Our policy was, "If the Canelas can't have them, and we can do without, we will."

We did bring in things essential for our translation work like a tape recorder, camera, and lots of books, and writing materials. And, since we were the only modern medical "doctors" we brought in cases of soap and modeled good hygiene. We boiled our water for drinking and recommended this to the Canela, especially in the beginning of the rainy season when the creeks ran brown, and the entire village suffered from diarrhea. We brought in hundreds of kilos of medicine and freely treated people through prayer and modern medicine for every type of disease. In these ways too, we modeled love, praying that people would focus on our message of God's love for them, and not be distracted by our foreignness.

But today we live among Canadians, non-Christians as well as fellow believers and are a part of the Canadian church. God has a message of love for our non-Christian neighbours, co-workers, and schoolmates. I wonder what distracts them from hearing His message?

Are some of us indulging in unbiblical lifestyles? Do some of us dogmatically present strongly held opinions on such topics as theology, government, politics, human rights, military action, pharmaceutics, big business, immigration, and temporary foreign workers, etc.?

What in our daily lives distracts from God's message? Is there anything about you and me that blinds, deafens, and sidetracks people from turning to God?

Eliminate distraction.

~~~~~~~~~~

Allah and Culturally Relevant Bible Translations

Some Christians have accused Wycliffe Bible Translators of producing "Muslim friendly" translations of the Bible in which *Allah* is used to refer to the Supreme Being and Creator of all. Critics point out the blasphemy of implying that Muslims and Christians worship the same Supreme Being. They claim that *Allah*, as described in the Qur'an, matches many of the descriptions of Satan in the Bible.

I have no idea how well informed these critics are, but I do know it is not the whole story. Consider these facts:

- Although the *Allah* described in the Qur'an does not match the description of the God in the Bible, when Bible translators use the term *Allah* it fully matches the description of God the Creator and Father of our Lord Jesus.
- The term *Allah* does not belong to Islam. It was used in writing more than a thousand years before Mohammed was born.
- Many, if not all, Christian Arabic translations of Scripture since the 8th century have used the term *Allah* for The Lord/God.
- There are 35 distinct Arabic languages in the world today. Many of them use *Allah* as the primary term to describe the Supreme Being.
- Christianity arrived in Malaysia and Indonesia at least 300 years before Islam arrived there and *Allah* was the term used to describe the God of the Bible.
- In Bible translations and other printed material in the Malay and Indonesian languages, the word *Allah* has been used continuously since the 1600s. *Allah* was used in the first printed edition of Matthew's gospel in Malay in 1629, only

eighteen years after King James Version of the English Bible was published.

- *Allah* was used in the complete Malay Bible published in 1733, two-hundred years *before* the founding of Wycliffe Bible Translators.
- Millions of Christians in many countries like Algeria, Egypt, Iraq, Jordan, Lebanon, Indonesia, Malaysia, Brunei, and other areas in Africa and Asia whose languages are in contact with Arabic people, have been using the word *Allah* as Creator God and the God and Father of the Lord Jesus Christ for many centuries.
- When in 2009 the Muslim dominated government of Malaysia passed a law prohibiting Christians from using the term *Allah* to refer to the Lord, the Creator God, Christians went to court and won the right to continue to use the word *Allah* on the basis that they had been using it long before Islam came to their country.

The Etymology of *Allah*

Even with this long history of widespread usage by Christians, many people still question the actual origin and meaning of the term *Allah*. This mystery vanishes, however, when you understand the way in which Arabic joins words together. The word *Allah* is a simple contraction of the Arabic article *al-* "the" with a second word *-ilah* "god/lord." When combined, they form the term *Allah* meaning "the God/the Lord" - that is, the one and only creator God of the universe. *Allah* is, therefore, the Arabic linguistic equivalent to the English word *God* or *the Lord.*

So, how do translators in other languages select a word for "God" that is culturally relevant, while remaining true to the full meaning of the Scriptures? In general, there are three ways Bible translators choose a term to use for the Supreme Being in their translation of the Bible.

1.   Use the name of the local high deity - the creator god. This was the method used when the gospel was brought to northern Europe. All the Teutonic/Germanic languages used the term *Gott* to describe the local deity. *Gott* was in common

use, and everyone knew what was meant although certainly not all the attributes of the Creator described in the Bible were present in the term *Gott*.

Wherever the local indigenous name for the high deity was adopted and then filled with all the true attributes of the God of the Bible, Christianity has flourished, and God is worshiped as *Gott, God, Tupan, Hananim, Magano, Imana, Yala, Koro, Io, Kalunga,* and many hundreds more.

By the way, *Gott* comes from the Teutonic tribal name, *Ghu-tio*; which comes from the old Germanic *Tiw,* (the name of the ancient German deity for which Tuesday was named); which comes from the Latin *Deus*; which comes from the old Latin, *Deiw-os.*

2.   Use a name already in use in neighboring languages. This was done when the gospel was brought to southern Europe. All the Romance languages, French, Spanish, Italian, Romanian, Portuguese, etc. used the word *Deus* or *Dios* from the Latin/Greek words *Deus/Theos*, which stems from the old Latin, *Deiw-os,* which comes from the ancient Indo-European word *Diw-os* meaning "to shine", the term used to refer to the chief sky-god, that is, the sun. So both the words *Deus* and *God* trace back to the name of the same pagan deity, the sun god.

3.   Use a name transliterated from one of the Semitic languages of the Middle East. In languages like Hebrew, Aramaic and all the other northern Semitic languages, the word *El* is used to describe the Supreme Being. Often this word is combined with a Hebrew adjective to describe some specific aspect of God.

For example, *El Olam*: Everlasting God; *El Roi*: God Who Sees; *El Elyon*: Most High God; *El Shaddai*: God Almighty; *El Gibhor*: Mighty God. The word *Elohim* (simply translated as God in English) occurs 32 times in the first chapter of Genesis: *Elah* is the Aramaic word for God used by the prophet Jeremiah. Lastly, all the southern Semitic languages, like Arabic, use *Allah* (a contraction of *al* and *ilah*) as the word for God/the Lord.

Thus, in the context of a mosque and the Qu'ran the term Allah refers to the Muslim understanding of the Supreme Being, while in the context of a church in southern Semitic culture, and the local translation of the Bible, the term Allah refers to the Christian understanding of the Supreme Being.

When my wife and I needed to choose a word for God when we translated the Bible for the Canela people of Brazil, we studied their creation myths. We found that the Canelas believed that after their Creator had made them, he abandoned them to fend for themselves as he ascended into the sky to shine as the sun. They called him *Pahpam*, meaning "Our Father."

Stuffing the Sausage Skin

Obviously, the meaning of the term *Pahpam* in very few aspects matched that of the Creator God of the Bible. But as we translated part of the Old Testament and most of the New Testament into Canela, we took this term—a nearly empty sausage skin—and stuffed it full of the solid meat of truth about God. The result is that now the Canela know that far from abandoning them, their Creator loves them and sent His Son to die so that they might become true sons of God and live with Him forever.

So, did we translate a "Canela friendly" Bible? Yes, of course, we did. That is the whole point of translating into another language and culture! Are *Pahpam* to the Canelas and *God* to us the same Supreme Being? Yes, they are now, though at first *Pahpam* certainly was not.

That is the beauty of God's plan: to guide translators to produce language and culture-friendly translations of His Word so that all the peoples of the world can get to know Him and understand His message of life and hope.

~~~~~~~~~~

Bible Translation: More Complex Than You Think . . . Way More!

Ever since the time of the apostles, translation has held a

central role in Christian missions work. Jesus spoke and taught in the local language, Aramaic, while Greek was a more widely understood language in the surrounding regions. When the early Christians wanted to record the teachings of Jesus, they first had to translate His words so that their work could reach the broadest possible audience. This makes Christianity unique, in that all major world religions have preserved the words of their founders in the very language in which they spoke them, all except Christianity.

Matthew, Mark, Luke, and John were the first translators. They translated all the stories about Jesus, and all his teachings, from Aramaic to Greek. Ever since then, Bible translators have been translating from Greek into other languages.

Most North American Christians don't appreciate the fact that Christianity was started as a translated religion, and thrives only through translation into local languages. Nor do most people understand that the Gospel writers did not simply translate between two closely related languages such as English and French. Instead, they translated from Aramaic, a Semitic language like Hebrew and Arabic into Greek, an Indo-European language like French and Russian.

There is as much relationship between these two language families as there is between English and Mandarin Chinese. Besides that, they had to keep in mind they were translating from Jewish culture to Greco-Roman culture. Again, a huge difference since these cultures expressed the same concepts using different words and ideas.

Bible translation, therefore, is an extremely complex task, but one that God has blessed throughout the ages. My friend and Wycliffe colleague, Hart Wiens, is an expert in Bible translation. He is Director of Scripture Translations for the Canadian Bible Society and laid the groundwork for the translation of the Scriptures for the Kalinga people of the Philippines.

Hart Wiens wrote an article for the June 22, 2012, issue *of Christian Week*, quoting Lamin Sanneh, a former Muslim, which is excerpted here with permission.

Tackling Translation

In his widely acclaimed book, *Translating the Message*, Lamin Sanneh, professor of World Christianity and History at Yale University, wrote that, "The central and enduring character of Christian history is the rendering of God's eternal counsels into terms of everyday speech." This demonstrates that "God does not absolutize any one culture."

This is a radical departure from the tenets of the religion in which Sanneh grew up where authoritative communication from God was restricted to one language. Translation is key to the spread of Christianity.

Recently, though, disagreement over the faithful and sensitive treatment of certain key terms in a few situations where Islam is the dominant religion has sparked a controversy that has deeply touched the hearts of people engaged in and supportive of this work.

The controversy

While the U.S. branch of Wycliffe Bible Translators has been specifically named in this controversy, the issues raised have relevance for the broader translation community and for the Church.

The issue is how to translate familial terms for God as "Father" and Jesus as "Son" in languages where these terms are only understood biologically. If translators are not careful, serious misunderstandings arise about the nature of the Trinity. Unfortunately, literal renderings have mistakenly been understood by people with a Muslim background, to imply that God and Mary had a physical sexual relationship.

In these situations, translators struggle to find more accurate ways of communicating the true nature of the father and son relationship in the Trinity—a relationship of familial rather than biological intimacy.

The Response

About the time Hart wrote the article excerpted above, Wycliffe presented all their Bible translation policies and practices for a formal review led by respected theologians, biblical scholars, translators, linguists, and missiologists from the global Church and conducted under the auspices of the World Evangelical Alliance. After nearly a year of study and discussion, the review panel came up with a list of recommendations. They approved most of Wycliffe's policies and practices and gave helpful suggestions in the area of translating familial terms.

Dr. Freddy Boswell, President of SIL, Wycliffe's field partner wrote, "The independent review panel has done us a great service. The panel's recommendations have been adopted as SIL's standards for the translation of these familial terms when referring to God the Father and to the Son of God."

He goes on to say, "In reviewing this report, we recognize that SIL contributed to the controversy through our failure to communicate translation standards and practices clearly. We also recognize that our processes for monitoring translation of Divine Familial Terms have been inadequate. We apologize and will endeavor to correct these shortcomings. We are indebted to this WEA-facilitated panel for their excellent and thorough work on behalf of our organization and we reaffirm our commitment to accurate, clear and natural translation."

Wycliffe has given assurance that their personnel "are not omitting or removing the familial terms, translated in English as "Son of God" or "Father," from any Scripture translation. The eternal deity of Jesus Christ and the understanding of Jesus' relationship with God the Father must be preserved in every translation."

The Conclusion

Unless they have been personally involved in translating between utterly different languages and cultures, few people, even highly educated scholars, grasp the complexity inherent in translating the Bible. Consider, it is a huge document, written thousands of years ago by a wide variety of authors, for cultures that no longer exist. How to translate it accurately and meaningfully for the huge variety of cultures and languages, thousands of them, in the world today? Yet, that is what God has determined needs to be done. How else will there be some "from every tribe and language and nation" on earth to stand before His throne to worship Him?

The same Holy Spirit who inspired authors to write the Bible in the first place is there to help and guide in translating it into every language on planet Earth.

~~~~~~~~~~~

What Does "Thank you" Mean Anyway?

While translating the Bible with the Canela people of Brazil, my wife and I ran into a problem—we could not find a simple word or phrase for the concept carried in English by such words as gratitude, thanksgiving, grateful, thankful, and "Thank you."

Were the Canelas never grateful? we wondered. *And if they were, how did they express it?* We knew we had to do some research to find a solution. After all, thanksgiving is a major, basic concept in God's Word.

We asked ourselves, "What is implied when we say, 'Thanks'?"

Here is the list we came up with:

- I had a need—something I didn't have, or some action I could not do by myself.
- You had what I needed.
- You became aware of my need.
- You realized you could help me by supplying my need.
- You made an effort to give me what I needed.
- What you gave to me, or did for me, was good; it perfectly fit my need.
- I am now satisfied and happy.
- I feel a sense of debt to you.
- I acknowledge what you did by saying something to you.

Once we compiled the list we saw immediately how Canelas expressed gratitude. When receiving something they sometimes said, *"Ita ahna, impej,"* meaning, "It's right, it's good," expressing #6 on the list. When they were very pleased with our gift they would say, *"Ate ima hor pyren, ijakry!"* meaning "Because you gave it to me, I am happy!" expressing #7.

Other cultures focus on different aspects. For instance, Brazilians say *"Obrigado"* meaning "I am obligated to you" expressing #8.

Several cultures say, "I'm terribly sorry" which focuses on #5, the fact that you freely took the time and trouble to meet their need.

Human Babies: The Most Self-Centreed Beings on Earth

Expressing gratitude does not come naturally to us. Not surprising since we start life as babies—the most self-centreed beings on earth. It is all about *our* food, *our* comfort, and *our* pleasure. As small children, we have to learn that it's *not* all about us. We need to learn to be aware of others, to share toys, to await our turn, and to be aware of the rights of other people.

Children need lots of help to learn to feel and express gratitude. Parents know how hard it is to teach their children to say "Thank you." They constantly model gratitude by saying, "Thank you," when a child does even the smallest thing voluntarily or in response to a request.

Selfish ingratitude has a history as long as the age of the universe. It started with Satan, the most impressive, beautiful and powerful angel created by God. Satan owed everything he was and all his abilities to God who created him, yet was not thankful. He refused to acknowledge God as superior, the Great Provider, and instead launched an angelic rebellion to usurp the throne of God.

God exiled Satan to earth, where for thousands of years he has polluted the minds and will of people with this same ungrateful attitude. The apostle Paul mentions this to the church in Rome as he describes people under the power of Satan, ". . . they neither glorified God nor gave thanks to Him . . . " Romans 1:21 (NIV).

Imagine putting yourself out to help a friend, doing things for him, and giving him what he needs, but he takes it all for granted, never expressing gratitude. How long is your friendship going to last? In the same way, how can our relationship with God grow and strengthen if we take Him for granted and fail to thank Him for all that He has done, and is doing for us?

Our Sin: Taking God's Blessings for Granted

Submerged in an ungrateful culture, it is so easy to take for granted all the things we got as gifts from God—many of them through little work or effort of our own. Think of our physical life and health, our spiritual life and growth, our families and friends, our freedom and affluence, the abilities and opportunities open to us, and especially God's Word translated in our own language. Millions of people in developing countries would give their right arm to have what we take for granted.

How can we be more thankful? We could start by taking our eyes off those few people who are richer than we are, and compare ourselves to the 90 percent of the world's people who, through no fault of their own, are much poorer.

We could continue to compare ourselves with those who are sick and without health care, those who live under oppressive regimes, who have lost their friends and families, who have never had a chance to learn to read, and who have no Bible in their language.

We could share what we have been given with others who are in greater need than we are.

Unless we regularly thank and praise God for all that He provides for us, and then go on to share our blessings with others, our ingratitude will lead to increasing selfishness, a hardening of our hearts, and eventually a ruined relationship with the Great Provider.

Canela Christians love to sing a hymn to Jesus with the line, "*Acator pyren, me ijakryti!*" meaning "Because you came, we are very happy." Or "Thank You for coming to earth!"

Jesus the Saviour was God's greatest gift to humanity—well worth thanking Him for and sharing with others.

~~~~~~~~~~~

There's Just No Word for It

"But what if there is no word for it in the language?" someone will inevitably ask during a discussion about Bible translation. Usually the "it" people ask about is some abstract biblical term like "faith" or "redemption" but the "it" could be something quite concrete.

No Wheat

We ran into this problem when we were translating the passage in which Jesus was teaching the need to sacrifice ourselves to accomplish a greater good, "Unless a kernel of wheat falls to the ground and dies, it remains only a single seed. But if it dies, it produces many seeds" John 12:24 (NIV).

The Canela language of Brazil has no word for wheat since wheat does not grow well in the jungle. The Canelas, however, plant rice which looks a lot like wheat and acts exactly the same. So we translated the passage, "Unless a kernel of rice is planted in the ground and dies, it will remain only a single seed. But if it dies, it produces many seeds." Bible translators call this "the principle of using a cultural equivalent in place of a lexical equivalent."

No Sheep

We did the same thing when we translated the passage where Jesus crossed the lake of Galilee and approaching the far shore, he sees a great crowd of people milling around. Mark reports, "He had compassion on them, because they were like sheep without a shepherd" Mark 6:34 (NIV).

Since sheep are unknown among the Canela, the only domesticated animals being pigs, chickens, and dogs, we asked our Canela translation helpers, "What is there in your village that is lost without a caretaker?" They talked among themselves for a while and came up with an illustration that seemed to fit.

So we translated the passage, "they were like baby chicks without a mother hen." This was a perfect simile since without the mother hen nearby her chicks are lost, wandering all over the yard cheeping piteously.

No Sacrifice

Not long afterward, however, we had another problem involving sheep. John the Baptist was in the Jordan, baptizing people when, suddenly he saw Jesus coming and shouted out, "Look, the Lamb of God, who takes away the sin of the world!" John 1:29 (NIV).

A lamb is a sheep, but we could not use the chicken metaphor, since this time the lamb had nothing to do with being lost without a shepherd, but with the God-given command to kill a lamb and present it to God as a burnt sacrifice to cover the sins of the people. For two-thousand years the Jewish people had regularly sacrificed an innocent lamb to cover their sins, which, of course, was a picture of Jesus, the Lamb of God, who came to die, not just to cover the sins of all humanity temporarily, but to take them away forever.

I explained to our translation helpers how the Jewish people would slit the throat of a lamb, pour out its blood, butcher the carcass and then put it on a fire to burn it up. They corrected me saying, "No, no! Not "burn it up" but "roast it." How can you eat if it is burnt up?"

When I explained that the lamb was not for eating, but for burning, they were upset and confused. "Don't tell us any more stories about those crazy Jews; they don't even know what to do with a nice little lamb."

I understood why they were so confused. The concept of ritual sacrifice is unknown among the Canelas. They killed animals only to eat them, unless, of course, it was a dangerous animal, like a poisonous snake.

Since this was a major translation problem, we sent out newsletters to our supporting partners back home explaining it and asking them to pray. And we kept on translating, but each time we came to a passage that talked about Christ's sacrifice of Himself, we put it aside.

No Solution?

It was years later that we discovered a solution that God had embedded in the Canela culture centuries before.

~~~~~~~~~~

The Solution God Provided

How were we going to translate "Jesus is the Lamb of God" when the Canelas have no concept of sacrifice? How will they ever understand the idea of Jesus offering Himself to suffer the death humanity deserved?

Here's the rest of the story. Years passed as we translated other parts of the Bible, developed more learn-to-read materials, and prayed for a solution. The solution came when we returned from furlough in Canada, arriving in the middle of a major Canela festival.

The Festival

Hundreds of Canelas were gathered in the central hub of the village. About fifty young women stood shoulder to shoulder in a long line singing and dancing. The dance and song leader shook his rattle energetically, stomping out a good strong beat. Dozens of young men, their bodies painted in red and black, waved spears and clubs above their heads as they danced and showed themselves off to the young women. The old men sat in small groups, smoking, chewing and spitting. The older women sat behind the line of dancing women, and gossiped. I dashed here and there taking pictures. It was so good to be back!

Suddenly I noticed one of the elders jogging very determinedly from his house down one of the radial paths towards the centre hub. He was chanting loudly, and carried a muzzle-loading shotgun. When he arrived in the midst of all the merriment, he pointed his gun into the air and BLAMM!!

Instant silence. Everyone stopped and looked at him. He handed his gun to another elder, then, waving his clenched fists, he started to rant. I heard words like Lazy! Good for nothing! Disobedient! and I thought, *Oh, oh, some of this old uncle's nephews are really going to get it.* I had seen this ritual before.

The Punishment

At the end of his rant, he stepped into the crowd, grabbed one of his nephews by the arm and pulled him back to the open centre where everyone could see him. He said nothing, just looked the young man in the eye, then stomped heavily on his foot. The nephew winced and limped away.

I had seen uncles punishing nephews in a variety of ways, by lifting them up by their hair, rubbing peppers in their mouths and even putting stalks of sawgrass in their nephew's armpit and jerking it out. Ouch!

I had witnessed this traditional Canela method of publicly shaming and punishing on other occasions. But then something happened that I had never seen before.

The Substitute

The uncle had just led another nephew out of the crowd and was about to yank him off his feet by the hair, when suddenly a young woman ran up out of the dancing line, stepped in front of the nephew and faced the uncle.

The uncle looked her in the eye and grabbing the hair on both sides of her head, yanked several times upwards, making her jump. She winced in pain and walked teary-eyed back to her place in the dancing line where she stood rubbing her scalp, while the young man turned and walked freely back to his group. After that, no matter who the uncle tried to punish, or how he tried to punish him, some young woman ran out of the dancing line and took the punishment for him.

I knew what the relationship was between each of these young men and the young women. It was called the *kritxwy* [kreet-TSWUH] meaning ritual substitute—a person assigned to stand in for someone else. Every Canela has a *kritxwy* partner. Even I have one.

Once during a ceremony on the central plaza, it was my turn to sing, and I forgot some of the words of the long song. When I faltered, I stepped aside and my *kritxwy* stepped up and finished my song.

Over the years I had seen this happen scores of times in all sorts of social situations, but I had never seen a *kritxwy* take the punishment for their partner. But when I saw that, I couldn't wait to get back to the translation desk and translate all those passages that, for years, I had put aside.

The Result

The next day I came to the central plaza and told the group of elders gathered there, *Jeju Crixto pe mepahkritxwy, ne tamari mepancwyrjape ty!* "Jesus Christ is our Kritxwy and it was He who died in our place!"

When we began using this term to describe Jesus and what He had done for them, it was like a bomb went off in the village. The Canelas suddenly began to realize who Jesus was, and what He had done for them, and many decided to follow Him.

God Himself had embedded this redemptive analogy right in the culture and rituals of the Canelas many centuries before. He did this because He has always loved the Canelas and wanted them to know Him.

And now you know the rest of the story.

~~~~~~~~~~

A Bible Translator at His Personal Devotions

You know how irritating it is to have someone interrupt a good conversation. Worse yet is to have the person you are talking with suddenly stop listening and write a reminder to himself, answer a text message or take a cell phone call. It tends to throw the conversation right off track! Sometimes I can't even remember the unforgettable story I was telling!

Unfortunately, I have done the same thing to God, especially during the decades that my wife and I were fully focused on translating the Scriptures for the Canela people of Brazil.

One morning, I started reading 1st Corinthians in my personal devotions. We had not yet translated this book. By the time I was done I had produced the notes below:

1Corinthians 1:1-2

"From Paul, who was called..." Thank You, Lord for calling me to translate Your Word for the Canelas. Help me do a good job.

[Mmm, 'called,' I'd better use 'chose' or the Canelas will think Paul was far away and God had to shout for him. On the other hand that was sort of what happened on the Damascus road... well I'd better get back to reading.]

"...called by the will of God to be an apostle..." Yes, Lord, it was Your will, Your eternal plan that worked in Paul's life, just as it does in mine.

[Wait a minute, does 'will of God' refer to both his calling and his appointing or just to the latter? Is this going to make a difference in Canela? Also, I need to change the passive 'I was called' to the active 'God called me.' Sure wish Canela had a passive tense. Oh well.]

"...and from our brother Sosthenes..." Hey, that is great Lord. Paul and one of his converts writing to other converts. I'd love to do that someday for the Canela.

['brother', need to make sure that I add 'because of Jesus' or something like that to keep people from thinking he was Paul's biological brother. I suppose he was a Greek, need to check on that, can't have Paul saying 'we' meaning 'we Jews' if Sosthenes is a Greek and a co-author. I suppose he is a co-author, or is he just adding his name to include him in the greetings? Oh boy, need to check on that too.]

"...to the church of God..." Right! It is Your church, Lord. Not Paul's church or some preacher's or some denomination's. Help the folks at home to understand that Lord. The church is Yours. The Canela church, whenever it comes into being, will also be Yours.

[Hey, wait a minute, I can't leave the salutation and address till this far along! I'd better move at least this part of verse two up to verse one and start, 'Hello, you who are God's group in Corinth, I am Paul... Oh, another thing, I'd better put Corinth city, or else they might think it is Corinth land.']

"...to those sanctified in Christ, called to be saints..."
Thank You, Father, for making me holy and separate, setting me apart for Yourself through the work of Your Son, and calling me to live that way daily. Fill me anew with Your Spirit so I may have the power to live as I should.

[I wonder, hopefully, he is using the term 'Christ' simply as a name, not to refer specifically to Jesus as the Jewish Messiah. Have to check that out. Also, are 'sanctified' and 'called to be saints' slightly different concepts? Does 'call' refer to a one-time event in the past, and 'sanctified' as the continuing consequences? Or is Paul just using two related terms as a form of emphasis? Sure hope it is the latter, would be lots easier to translate!]

Whoops, sorry Lord.

"...together with all people in every place..." That is inspiring! The Church had already spread all over the world, and even more so now. Lord, help me to spread Your church

58

into these Canela villages too.

[I just remembered, the Jews often used the term 'place' to mean synagogue. If that is what Paul meant, I need to say, 'all people in every meeting place,' or 'wherever they meet' since in those days Christians didn't use a special building to meet in.]

"...both theirs and ours..." Thank You, Lord, for being the Lord of all of us. Older and younger Christians all have the same Lord. And so do people of all races and languages - including the Canela.

[I do hope this term doesn't refer to 'their meeting place and our meeting place.' Grammatically it could. But surely the sense of the whole letter is unity among Christians. But better check that out too. Man, I'm not getting very far. Maybe I'd better go back to having my devotions out of Mark!]

Lord, I'm sorry. You must be getting ticked off at me. I keep interrupting our talk with work-related reminders to myself. Instead of focusing on listening to You and talking to You, I'm busy getting ready for the next translation project.

In this instance, please accept my desire to do excellent work as an incarnational form of worship. I do love You and want to worship You by doing my work to the best of the talents You have given me. Amen.

~~~~~~~~~~

Biased Bible Translators

I still consider myself a Bible translator, even though we completed our 22-year long task of translating the Scriptures into Canela several decades ago. I guess that is why I take offense when Bible translators blatantly mistranslate a passage to fit their own strong cultural bias—an unbiblical bias. I don't get angry at changes in wording where the full meaning is still preserved. I get upset when translators allow their own worldview to pervert the clear meaning of Scripture.

Bible Translation Basics

First some background. We all know that translation from one language, culture, and age into another is not a word-to-word process. Initially, translators need to distill the meaning from the source language—the language from which they are translating. Then, they translate that meaning into the target language—the language into which they are translating.

This second stage of the translation process is wide open for the translator to skew the meaning to fit his or her own mindset. That is why highly trained consultants and experienced translation checkers surround all Wycliffe Bible translators and use multiple review processes to make sure everything we translate is true to the original meaning.

For example, since wheat did not exist in Canela culture, there was no word for it. So, when my wife and I needed to translate the word "wheat," we used the Canela word for "rice." Using a cultural equivalent term was not an act of sin, but the use of a perfectly acceptable Bible translation technique. The meaning was fully preserved by using a more culturally relevant word.

Form versus Function

Translators have been doing this for centuries. For instance, the translators of the 1611 King James Authorized Version rendered James 1:23 "... a man beholding his natural face in a glass..." Yet, the original Greek word described a reflecting surface made not from glass, but from polished metal, usually silver, copper, or tin. This technique is called "different in form but serving the same function" and has been used by Bible translators for centuries all over the world.

Bias Against Women

I have long been offended, however, by how translators have handled a very familiar verse, " The Lord gave the word: great was the company of those that published it." Ps 68:11 (KJV). Yet, the Hebrew says *hammebasseroth tsaba rab*; "...of the *female* preachers there was a great host."

The Hebrew term without any doubt refers to women preachers. But only three out of the nine popular English versions on my computer reflect the fact that these preachers were women. Six out of nine translators for English versions choose generic terms such as *host, multitude, army, crowd*, and *company* instead of the more accurate terms like *women preachers*, or *female proclaimers*.

Why did these translators hide the fact that the original Hebrew unequivocally meant *women* preachers? It was the translators' own cultural bias against women preachers that led them to mistranslate in this way. A mistranslation such as this that negatively impacts women in ministry really ticks me off! After all, women comprise over half of God's Church on earth.

A similar example is the Greek word *diakonos*, which is translated as *minister* or *leader* almost everywhere in the New Testament. But in Romans 16:1, eight out of ten English versions render the word *diakonos* not as *leader*, or *minister*, but as *servant* or *helper*. Why? The only reason is that the translators just could not bring themselves to use the word *minister* or *leader* of Phoebe, a woman.

The apostle Paul was not a despiser of women, but the secular Greek culture was. Paul consistently treated women as equal to men, contrary to the prevailing Greco-Roman culture.

But, a thousand years later, translators into English were so influenced by ancient Greco-Roman philosophy they re-interpreted the plain statements of Paul to fit their own unbiblical cultural bias. They allowed the pagan Greco-Roman worldview of women as being less than men to influence their translation of the Bible.

Their mistranslations have shaped the thinking of Christians ever since. If the Church is to fully obey the Great Commission, we need to let the truth of God's Word renew our mindsets, worldviews, and cultural biases.

~~~~~~~~~~

Get Rid of Traditions of Pagan Origin? Whoa! Not so Fast!

Each year as Halloween approaches the annual hue and cry begins among Christians to scrap any observance of this pagan, pre-Christian, and unbiblical celebration.

Whoa! Wait a minute!

First of all, you know that I am all in favour of Christians acting counter-culturally in some areas. After I took a swipe at materialism in one of my columns, a reader wrote saying she is going to start a Salmon Club, where Christians help each other to swim upstream, against the cultural current. I like that! Every Christian church should be a Salmon Club. To swim against the stream of unbiblical cultural practices is one of the Church's stated functions.

Echoes of Our Pagan Past

On the other hand, to simply research the history of something in our current culture, and scrap it if it is found to be of pagan, non-Christian origin, is ridiculous. Consider: The days of the week are named after pagan gods.

Saturday honours the Roman god *Saturn*. Sunday and Monday are named, of course, after *Sun* and *Moon*, both honoured by pagan Anglo-Saxon peoples. The other four days of the week honour four Norse gods, Tuesday: *Tiw*, the god of war; Wednesday: *Woden*, the high god; Thursday: *Thor*, god of thunder; and Friday: *Frigga*, the wife of *Woden*.

Five of the months of the year carry the names of pagan Roman gods:

January: *Janus*, the two-faced god, one looking back the other ahead; February: either from the god *Februus*, or from *februa*, the pagan festivals of purification celebrated in Rome during this month; March: *Mars*, the god of war; May: *Maiesta*, the goddess of honour and reverence; June: *Juno*, the chief goddess.

The name God can be traced back through Gott, Ghu-tio, Tiw, Deus, Deiw-os, to the Indo-European name Diw-os meaning "to shine", the term used to refer to the chief sky-god, that is, the sun. Does that make all God worshipers sun worshipers?

On the basis that it was a pagan celebration, the Puritans in the mid-1600s discarded all observance of Christmas, forcing people to work and expelling students who failed to come to school on Christmas Day. In America, even 200 years later, most Protestant groups still refused to celebrate Christmas. So should we, like they, replace all these names and terms because they have a non-Christian, pagan history? Of course not!

Everything Started as a Pagan Practice

Bible translators and cross-cultural missionaries know better than anyone else that every human being on earth is part of a group with a unique culture, its own social behaviour patterns, and distinctive worldview. Our languages reflect our cultures and our cultural histories. No worker from a reputable mission agency would walk into a foreign cultural situation and willy-nilly destroy or change anything that he or she suspected of being pagan. Hey, everything is pagan in a pagan society! Including the language and all its vocabulary!

No, what a missionary does is bring truth, biblical truth, into every situation. Through the Truth, God transforms a culture. As people read the Scriptures, God's Holy Spirit teaches them about Himself. This happened among the Canela people of Brazil among whom my wife and I worked as Bible translators for over 22 years.

The term *Pahpam* meaning "Father of us all" referred to the Deity who had made the Canelas and then went away to live far away up in the sky as the Sun and no longer concerned Himself with them. Canelas, therefore, rarely prayed to Him. Instead, through their ceremonies, they dealt with the ghosts of dead ancestors, and the spirits inhabiting animals or areas around them. When the Canelas began to read the Bible, they took the name *Pahpam* and stuffed the pagan term full of new

63

truth. *Pahpam* was not only their Maker/Father, but He is still present. He is not the sun; He made it. He had not abandoned them. He is not silent, but wants to speak to them through His Word, and loves them enough to send His Son to die for them so that they can be reconciled to Him.

So, What About Halloween?

That pagan festival was transformed, and for many decades across North America, it was a great time for kids to dress up in costumes, meet the neighbours, collect some candies, and have a good time.

In some areas, Halloween seems to be reverting to its pagan past as a high day in the evil, occult world. The time may come for Christians to start swimming upstream again. To join the Salmon Club and refuse to go along with the occult, the demons, evil spirits, ghosts, ghouls, and malevolent witches and wizards. These beings are real. Dressing up as one of them is not the same as dressing up as a fantasy figure like a Princess, Spiderman or Gandalf.

Halloween needs to be redeemed as a time of fun for kids and their parents. But let's not scrap it because of its pagan origin. Once we start on that road, where do we stop?

~~~~~~~~~~

The Profitable Interruption

It was a hot, still afternoon in the Canela village. I was hunched over my study table, deeply engrossed in thinking and praying through a long list of key biblical terms. How was I going to express in good Canela such terms as *Son of Man, Saviour, and Mediator*?

Suddenly the sound of many feet in the open porch area of our house drummed away the silence. Then the chant began. Many voices—strong men's voices—loudly singing a low-pitched chant, their feet stamping rhythmically on the hard packed dirt floor. Now what? Yet another interruption to my studies.

Discovering New Terms and Expressions

I had already discovered the Canelas had many ways to express mediating peace. One term meant "to set down water for each other." Picture the chiefs of two warring tribes coming together to make peace. Each brings a gourd of water and sets it down for the other to drink. Each then drinks from the gourd the other set down for him – somewhat like smoking the peace pipe among North American Indians. Except for one thing – with all the toxic plants available in the jungle, it would be very simple to poison the water. So drinking the water which the other chief brought was an act of faith and trust.

But I was still stuck on how to translate 1 Timothy 2:5 "There is one God and one *mediator* between God and mankind, the man Christ Jesus." I needed a good term for someone who made peace between two warring factions. I was confident I would find a good term for a peacemaking *mediator* since Canelas like peace. That's understandable since a small group could quickly exterminate itself if it allowed squabbles to escalate to killing.

Studies Interrupted

Meanwhile, outside the chant had grown louder and had taken on threatening overtones. I gave up my studies as a lost cause and joined the crowd. About 60 men, armed with spears and clubs, shouted their chant and stamped their feet. No good asking questions, no way to speak above that din. Then it got even louder and looking towards the central plaza, I saw why.

A similar sized group of men was approaching in a line abreast, also chanting and stamping. They held their spears and clubs horizontally at chest level in the way riot police hold their batons to shove back a rioting mob. The group in our house immediately ran out and arranged themselves in a solid line abreast, also punching forward with their clubs and spears held horizontally in both hands. I got well out of the way! The opposing group kept stomping closer and closer until the two lines were nose to nose, the fists holding spears and clubs nearly touching. Crowds of Canela men, women and children now surrounded the two groups of warriors. The two chants deafened us. Hundreds of stamping feet shook the ground.

Even though I was pretty sure this was yet another choreographed ritual to confirm Canela social values, it almost looked like a battle was just about to start. Just then two men stepped out of the encircling crowd. Decorated with pieces of cloth tightly tied around their bodies, arms, legs, and head, they spread their arms wide and subtly insinuated themselves in between the two lines of shouting, stamping, threatening warriors. They gently pushed the warrior lines farther apart, then turned them to form one group. Soon the chants died down, the angry expressions softened, and the spears and clubs were lowered. Then, singing a new and happier song, they all marched off to the central plaza to continue the peace-making festival.

A Culturally Fitting Term at Last!

I couldn't wait to find out what the Canelas called these peacemakers! The term was *mepajaxorcate*, "one who hangs us together." The image is of someone taking two separate items, such as pineapples, and tying them together with a piece of string, then looping the string on a peg in the wall. The pineapples can't help but hang closely together. I had my term for mediator! Jesus is our *mepajaxorcate*. He is the one who hangs people and God closely together.

Right now, in nearly 2,000 cultures and languages, translators continue to search for, and find, just the right term to use for any of hundreds of key terms. Two thousand other cultures and languages, all rich in metaphors and redemptive analogies, are still waiting for someone to come to start translation work.

Every few days, somewhere in the world, a Bible translation program starts in a new language. May that rate speed up even more, until there is not a language in the world still waiting for the Bible translation process to start.

In the end, it's not about vivid metaphors or clear analogies. It is not even about hundreds of millions of people who do not have even one word of the Bible translated into their languages.

It is about God who wants people to know He loves them, and that He wants them to hang closely together with Him for all eternity.

~~~~~~~~~~

Jack, Your Translation Has Too Many Words

My missionary friend frowned as he read my translation of the gospel of Luke, looked up and said, "Jack, your translation is good, but it has too many words."

I remembered that incident years later when I saw the movie *Amadeus* in which Emperor Joseph II criticized Mozart, "Your work is ingenious, but there are too many notes."

My friend and I were translators in distantly related indigenous Brazilian languages. With effort, we could somewhat read each other's translation. I was a member of Wycliffe Bible Translators, and he belonged to another mission organization. Our training in Bible translation principles had been quite different. We both, of course, insisted on accuracy, faithfully reflecting the content of the text from which we translated. But we used different standards for judging a passage to be well translated.

Ask the Right Questions

After translating a passage, my translator friend would ask himself, "Can this verse be understood?" if the answer was yes, he would go on to translate the next verse.

I asked myself, "Can this verse be *mis*understood?" If the answer were no, I would go on to the next verse, but if yes, I would retranslate it until the answer was no.

I learned this concept from CS Lewis who taught me much about writing for clarity, first by the example of his own works and then by the advice he gave to fellow writers.

"Readers do not start by knowing what you mean. Most will

misunderstand if you give them the slightest chance. It is like driving sheep down the road; if there is any gate open to the left or the right, they will go into it."

When I was translating, and now whenever I write, I keep asking, "Is there any open gate, a word, expression, or construction that would cause a reader to go astray?"

My friend's mission organization had teams of missionaries living in all the villages for which he was translating, and, as he put it, "If there is any misunderstanding, they will explain and teach the readers."

Jo and I knew there was no guarantee that there would be any missionaries in any of the Canela villages to "explain and teach the readers" so we determined that the Canela translation needed to stand on its own merits with all gates closed, even if it took more words to close them.

Using More Words to Avoid Confusion

And we did use many more words. Take, for instance, a basic gospel verse like John 3:16. In English the number of words ranges from 25 (KJV) to 31 (CEV) to 40 (MSG). The Cakchiquel translation has 62 words, and the Canela translation we did has 66 words. Here's why we had to use more words:

world: Canelas would take this as God loving the land on which they lived, the environment. And God does love His natural creation, but the focus is on "all the people who live on earth" (1 English word to 6 Canela words)

gave: Implied in this word is that God "sent him towards us into this world where we live," (1 word to 9)

son: Since Canelas do not talk about themselves in the third person, we had to put this into the form "I who am his Son," (1 word to 4)

believe: This term implies more than just mental assent but having a behavior-changing effect. Therefore the form, "he empowers himself with" (1 word to 4) *perish*: What is implied in this term is to "die and stay dead and exist forever far away from God" (1 word to 11)

everlasting life: Canela makes contrasts explicit, "In favorable comparison (to the previous situation) they return to life and live alongside God forever" (2 words to 12)

And that's how eight keywords in English turned into 50 words in Canela.

Those 42 extra words are gate closers and essential to keep readers from straying from the path of truth.

Mozart's compositions were criticized for having too many notes because they were dense and complex.

Our translation was criticized for having too many words because it was simple and clear. It was those extra words that made things clear and closed the gates of confusion.

~~~~~~~~~~

How the Canelas Understand the Good News

Fifty years ago, my wife and I, with our three pre-school daughters, accepted the invitation to live among Brazil's Canela people in their main village. We immediately began to learn their culture and language. Our training had prepared us for many things, but even so the Canelas surprised us with their highly effective economic system.

We didn't expect to see money since it was a four-day round-trip on foot to the nearest store, but thought there would be bartering—exchanging one kind of good for another—such as a set of bone tipped arrows for a haunch of deer meat. Instead, we soon learned that the economic system was credit based. Meticulous records were kept, not on paper but in Canela brains. Yes, every Canela remembered a record of debts owed to them and debts they owed to others.

We should not have been so surprised. A barter system depends on people producing things that are different from those others produce. But every Canela family produced the same things as every other Canela family. Every family had hunters, water carriers, basket weavers, woodchoppers, gardeners, and cooks.

What they did not have, however, was an effective way to preserve fresh food. When a hunter returned with a deer, he knew his family could never eat it all before it spoiled. Everyone else knew this too. So other hunters would come and ask for a piece of meat, saying, "When I next kill a deer, I'll pay you back." Okay, no problem.

Our North American culture uses the same credit system when a neighbour is baking a cake and knocks on your door to borrow a cup of sugar. The Canela system, however, covered everything, not just material things but also time and effort. Twenty men would work for days to help one family cut house building poles and to construct the house, knowing the next time any of them needed help in a building project, they could get it from the family they had helped.

So what happens if a hunter has a crippling accident and he cannot pay a debt? No problem. The debt passes on to the hunter's extended family: a brother or other male relative takes on the debt. Do this year after year, and you have a fully functioning credit-based economic system that touches every aspect of life. Although money is now more commonplace, much of the current Canela economic system still is on credit.

We used this cultural practice in our Bible translation to make the Good News clear. In some sense, we human beings are in debt to God because of our disobedience to Him. Check out a parable about this in Matthew 18:23-35. We can't pay the debt ourselves, nor can any of our extended family since we are all in the same fix. But God had mercy on us and sent Jesus, who called himself *The Son of Man* meaning "the one who became human like you."

The Canelas call Jesus *Mepahaka*, "Our Older Brother." The sin debt we could not pay passed on to our older brother, Jesus, who paid it with His own life. Our debt is paid, we are forgiven, and we are free.

Isn't it great to see how God prepared the Canelas to understand the Good News by embedding this illustration in their own culture? It is what missiologists call a "Redemptive Analogy."

It is just one more way that helps Canelas understand that the God of the Bible is not a foreign God, but the One they recognize as their own Creator, their own Heavenly Father. That's why they talk about Him as Pahpam, Our Father. And the Canela Bible is called Pahpam Jarkwa (God's Word).

Let's keep praying that God's Spirit will guide every cross-cultural missionary to discover the analogies to redemption that are embedded in every culture. God invented languages, He invented cultures too, and made sure that His message of love was implanted in each culture.

~~~~~~~~~~

But How Do You Know If These Bible Translations Are Accurate?

Although I didn't know what to expect at my first writer's conference, I was surprised, pleased, and the first in line when a professional editor offered to critique our manuscripts. I gave her a tear sheet of a 2,500-word article I had written and which a magazine had published the month before.

"Every paragraph of your article throbbed with passion which made it publishable," she told me the next day, "but here's how you could have improved it," and handed it back covered with red scribbles.

As we sat together at lunch to go through the manuscript line by line, I mined the corrections and picked her brain, meticulously writing down every comment in my notebook. When we finished, I told her, "When I saw all those corrections I thought I had made hundreds of errors. But I hadn't. I just made half a dozen errors hundreds of times."

It was a most satisfying and productive lunch. I learned so much, and I told her so. She enjoyed it too, saying, "I was afraid you might get defensive and argue with me over every correction, but you are lapping this up which makes it fun. If you keep that attitude, you will improve and become a good writer."

The experience of having my writing thoroughly checked and corrected by a professional editor prepared my wife and me for plunging into translating the Bible into Canela where we leaned heavily on translation consultants to help us check, not just every line, but every phrase and word of the translation.

The Bible Translator

Every translator's theology, beliefs, orthodoxy, and Christian life are thoroughly checked before he is ever assigned to translate. But even so, can Bible translators push their own theological agenda, ride their doctrinal hobbyhorses, and translate passages to reflect their own biased opinions? Yes, they can! That is why trained translation consultants check every part of the translation to make sure that it is completely accurate, with nothing inserted or left out.

People often ask, "But how can translation checkers do this when they don't know the language of the translation they are checking?

Answer: Through back translation into the language of the consultant.

There are three ways for the translator to produce this back translation. Two easy ways—which are worthless—and one hard way—which is useful.

The Two Easy Ways

For example, the second part of Revelation 11:1, *"Rise, and measure the temple of God, and the altar, and them that worship therein."* is a very simple command.

One easy way is to simply translate idiomatically into fluent English, like this: *"Go, measure God's temple and altar and count the worshippers."* This is useless to the consultant since it gives him no idea how concepts like *temple, altar,* and *worship*

72

are expressed in the target language.

The other easy way to back-translate is to simply do it word for word, like this example from the Canela language of Brazil:

"Attention, stand, go and with it, something-smoke-sweet-burning-thing that and our-inclusive-Father-about-they-themselves-into-their-ear-thing-house, with measure and they, our-inclusive-Father-like-people those count." This is practically unintelligible, and also of no use to the consultant.

The One Right Way

The third, and more difficult way is like walking on a slippery rail fence: lean too far to one side and the translation falls into being too idiomatic, too far to the other and it falls into literalism. Staying on the fence produces something a bit more useful like this:

"Listen, stand up and go and measure the thing for burning stuff to make sweet-smelling smoke, and measure the house of the place where they meditate on Our Father and count those people who love Our Father."

This back translation gives the consultant some idea of the term for *altar, temple, worship, and God.* Every verse of Scripture is back-translated and checked in this way.

By the way, currently, over 500 Wycliffe personnel serve as trained translation checkers and consultants to thousands of Bible translators all over the world.

~~~~~~~~~~

How Do You Know If the Readers Understand the Translation?

It's one thing to make sure the consultant is satisfied the Bible translation is accurate, but quite another to find out if the readers understand the translation. This part of the checking procedure is equally important, and a lot more fun.

The Process

The translator and the consultant are joined by an intelligent, fluent speaker of the target language, one who has never read or heard the Bible passage being checked.

The consultant asks a question which the translator repeats in the language of the translation helper. The translator listens carefully to the helper's answer which he then translates for the consultant.

The answer usually shows how well the indigenous co-worker understands the passage. What he understands, however, is sometimes strangely different from what the passage was supposed to say.

The Fun Part

When a translation consultant and I checked the rather simple story of the conversion of Saul in Acts 9, a highly intelligent and excellent Canela storyteller helped us. He couldn't read and had never heard of Saul before, so I read the passage to him. Then the consultant asked a question which I interpreted.

"Why did Saul become blind?" I expected our helper to say "God blinded him," or "The bright light from heaven blinded him." Instead, he said, "He banged his head on the road when he fell down."

Huh? My translation said, "He fell to the ground." No mention of his head, let alone of banging it. More questions got the answer. Once upon a time, a man in the Canela village had fallen out of a tree, hitting his head on the hard ground and was blinded for a while. Every villager knew the story.

I had to change the translation to "God blinded Saul," making the information explicit.

Where Did He Get That Idea?

Another question, "Why didn't Saul eat or drink =during those days in Damascus?" I expected, "He abstained from eating food to show God he was sorry for how badly he had treated the believers." Instead, he answered, "Because he had suffered a bad fall, and he was obeying the food restrictions. How else could he expect to regain his sight?"

I should have known. Canelas believe that in addition to medicines, recovery depends on the sick person, along with his closest blood relatives, restricting themselves to eating only certain kinds of foods or abstaining from food entirely. So I had to change the translation to make clear that it wasn't his obedience to the food taboo rules, but that God healed him after Saul repented.

Executioners in their Underpants

One of our Bible translating colleagues works with an indigenous group in southern Mexico. The story of the stoning of Stephen in Acts 7:57-58 was being checked with two men who often went hunting.

When they got to the part about taking off the clothes, the consultant expected to hear their interpretation as "They took off their coats and outer robes so they would be free to pick up and throw heavy stones." Instead, they said, "Oh, we do that too. When we shoot a deer, we take off our clothes before we butcher the carcass to avoid getting blood on them."

They thought that the stone throwers stripped down to their underpants to avoid getting Stephen's blood on their clothes. Another helper thought the clothes belonged to Stephen, the executioners stripping him naked before executing him, in the same way as had been done with Jesus a few months before.

Building on a Rock? Not Very Smart!

Our Canela translation helpers were totally confused when we began to translate the story of the wise man building on a rock and the foolish man building on the sand. Canelas build their villages on packed sand or sandy soil mixed with red clay. The only rock in the area is volcanic, very sharp, and painful to walk on. They would never dream of building a house on rock. And how could they dig holes in rock for house poles?

We had to abandon the sand and rock metaphor. We could choose to translate more generically, "The wise man built on a safe place, far away from where the river might flood the house. The foolish man built it in the path of the flood water."

Or we could switch completely to a Canela cultural metaphor. "The wise man cut down all the tall trees around his house, but the foolish one left them to stand. Then the wind came up and blew down some trees, but no falling tree could reach the wise man's house. Some trees, however, fell on the foolish man's house and crushed it."

(The elements we eventually used were solid red clay versus loose, dry sand.)

Conclusion

People automatically interpret everything in Scripture by their personal or cultural experience. It is not enough just to learn the language; the translator also needs to understand the cultural interpretations that the indigenous people are likely to make. And even then every passage needs to be checked with probing questions.

Yes, it's a lot of work, but God's Word is worth it.

~~~~~~~~~~

Administration and Quality Production

High Standards When Lives are at Stake

Missionary aviation mechanics are fanatics. They are intolerant, extreme, and I love it. Hey, my family and I flew over hundreds of miles of trackless jungle in those planes! It gave me great peace that the mechanics cut no corners. When, after a certain number of hours, an engine was due for an inspection, that plane was out of service, the engine inspected inside and outside, up and down, and every other way. I hope my doctor is as thorough when doing my annual physical checkup!

Those high aircraft maintenance standards were set by the manufacturer, the Brazilian government, and JAARS, Wycliffe's technical partner organization. The standards and procedures were all clearly stated in written policies. They were, no doubt, also fixed in the heads and hearts of the mechanics. But that was not all.

There was also an administrative structure in place to make sure the policies and procedures were adhered to. It reminds me of the administration adage, "What is INspected gets done, not what is EXpected." This is true in every human endeavour, even in missions, from servicing aircraft engines to producing Bible translations.

High Standards When Souls are at Stake

As Bible translators we were very much aware of Wycliffe's high standards for Bible translation. By the written policies, my wife and I needed to demonstrate certain levels of knowledge of the Bible, of linguistics, of culture, and of course, of proficiency in the language into which we were translating the Word. We also needed to demonstrate that the national translators with whom we worked were gifted in the use of their own language, that they knew how to think objectively about their language, and that they complemented my wife and me in the areas where we were weak—just as we complemented them.

Who made sure that all this was, in fact, the case? Well, my wife and I were highly motivated to produce the very best translation of which our team was capable. We had been well trained. And we were surrounded by a band of experienced consultants. This group of experts stood ready to help and advise in every aspect of our work: in linguistics, in cultural anthropology, in literacy, in translation, in Scripture use, etc.

Inspectors Essential

But motivation, training and consultant resources were not enough to assure a high-quality translation. There was also an administration that made sure the written standards, policies and procedures were being followed and that the desired quality was being attained.

Unless a consultant checked out and approved a publication, it was not printed. Unless the translation passed all the tests, it never saw the light of day in print or audio. In the end, it was not the written policies that kept the standards high. Nor was it our own fluctuating human motivation. Nor was it the training in workshops and seminars, nor the consultants' impassioned speeches on the importance of high standards. No, in the end, it came down to capable, well-trained, authorized administrators doing their job.

Now, decades after we completed the translation program, some things have changed. The standards and policies are no longer in paper manuals, but online where they are easily updated, searched and read. Translators from a growing number of countries and a wide variety of cultures now bring their unique skills and backgrounds to the task. Many are mother-tongue translators, translating into their own language.

But other things have not changed. Translators are still motivated from within to do a good job. Consultants are still checking and preaching quality. And, all over the world, in every case where field leaders and their administrators "govern diligently" in the sense of Romans 12:8, quality standards continue to be met. Qualified administrators, both at home and on the field, are the key to quality missions work.

Section Three: What God is Doing to Accelerate Bible Translation

Axe Head and Handle: A Vital Partnership

No missionary, no matter how intelligent and well educated, can accurately translate the Bible without constant feedback and input from at least one fluent, well-acculturated speaker of the target language.

For Jo and me to translate the Bible without a fluent speaker of the Canela as a constant partner would be like chopping wood with only an axe handle.

That is why, as soon as we arrived in the Canela village in Brazil, we prayed, and looked for Canela people who would help us learn the language, so we could analyze it and develop a writing system. After that, we looked for Canela people who were great storytellers and communicators, so we could train them and work with them as partners to translate God's Word into Canela. Bible translation was our main task since it is closest to God's own heart. At least that is what I understand David to say in Psalm 138:2, when he writes, "You have magnified Your word above all Your name" (NKJV).

The Training of Jaco

After our first few years of living in the main Canela village, we noticed a new face. Jaco, a young man in his late teens, had just returned from spending years in the big city. He was one of a group of Canelas who fled the village during an attempted massacre some years before we arrived.

He had attended school in the city and learned to read and write in Portuguese.

Jaco was bright and highly motivated to learn, so we invited him to work with us. Soon he learned to touch-type on our old Underwood typewriter and transcribed Canela stories and linguistic material faster and more accurately than I could. Unfortunately, having been away from the village for years, he was not as fluent in Canela, nor did he have as large a vocabulary as other young people his age. He was, therefore, unsuitable to partner with us in translation, and we kept praying and looking for someone else. God, however, had plans for Jaco.

After three months of special studies with other translators on the mission centre in the city, Jo and I returned to the village to discover that Jaco was "in seclusion." The village elders had decided that since he had not gone through the puberty rites as a child, he needed to go through them now, along with all the much younger boys.

I went to talk with him that same evening. I found him shut up alone in a small seclusion hut behind his relatives' house. Just like all the other initiates, he was not allowed to talk, work or sing—just silence, solitude and no physical labour.

We whispered to each other through the thatch. "I am so bored," he complained. "I wish I was back with you working on making reading books. But the elders won't let me go out or do any work."

He would be there for at least three months, receiving his food through a little slot in the palm-thatch wall. This is meant to teach young Canelas to get along without fire, clothing, covering or human companionship, and with only a small amount of water and food.

The hardships they endure during this time make them into true Canelas, able to sleep under any conditions and get along with only the very basic necessities of life.

Jaco Becomes a Sharp Axe Head

The next day I asked permission to speak to the elders at their early morning council session. "Every evening, when you tell stories of the old days, I have heard you complain that the young people are not coming to listen. You worry that after you are dead, no one will remember the stories. I have been making books of a few of your stories. Would you like all your stories to be in books? If they were, your descendants could read them forever."

"Yes, that's true," the elders replied, "but we are too old to learn to write down our stories."

"But you could tell more stories to my tape recorder, and then someone else, like Jaco, could quietly listen to them with headphones and copy them on the typewriter. That way we could make books from them for your grandchildren to read."

They discussed it for a while and gave their verdict: "Listening to stories on the headphones doesn't make noise, and tap-tapping them on the typewriter isn't work, so go ahead and ask Jaco to do this."

A few nights later, Jaco began what turned out to be his formal education as a Bible translation partner. For three full months, he did nothing but listen to audio tapes of stories told by the best storytellers in the village.

In listening and typing the hundreds of pages of text, he developed a powerful vocabulary, an excellent sense of language style, and a deep appreciation for the subtleties of his own language. When he finally came out of seclusion, God had shaped him into an excellent Bible translation partner.

With Jaco's fluency in Canela fitted to our knowledge of the Bible and our access to translation consultants and other specialists, we became a perfect team—a sharp axe head fitted tightly to a strong handle. Twenty years later we completed the translation project of a 750-page partial Bible in the Canela language.

God is in Charge

That God was the One who prepared Jaco to work with us to translate God's Word for his people, became clear to me when I looked at the chronology of events. If the elders had put Jaco in seclusion during the three months we were away on the centre, none of his training would have happened. But God was in charge. He arranged it so that Jaco was in seclusion and ready for training the very week we returned. He chose Jaco and prepared him to be His servant together with Jo and me to give His Word to the Canelas in their own language.

God continues to choose and to prepare thousands of indigenous men and women all over the world. They are joining Bible translation teams in over 2500 different cultures in 170 countries.

Some indigenous translation partners, like our friend and co-worker Jaco, are fluent in their own language but have only a basic general education. Increasingly, however, in more developed countries, nationals on translation teams are better educated. Some are even linguistic geniuses, fluent in many languages, with Ph.D.s from prestigious universities.

No matter what their background, they have one thing in common: God Himself chose and prepared them to help accomplish His world goal—speakers of every language in the world hearing His good news in the languages each of them knows best.

Just as He prepares these axe heads, so He prepares the axe handles—the translators, consultants, and specialists in computers, in literacy, in anthropology, in funding, and management.

God's Spirit inspired people to write His Word, and now He is preparing people and helping them to translate His Word into every human language. God is the Principal Partner.

~~~~~~~~~~

When Work Gets Boring

Boring Monotony

"This is getting tedious," I said, scowling at the shoe box partly filled with slips of paper, and Canela word lists scattered over my work table.

I stood up, stretched, and muttered to myself, "Day after day, week after week, nothing but hours and hours of writing down words, and grammatical features on hundreds of little cards. This monotony is getting me down."

In comparison, learning to speak Canela was a lot of fun, even though I regularly got laughed at whenever I practiced a new expression. But writing words on little cards was demotivating.

I looked at the clear blue, dry-season sky and prayed, "Lord God, please help me. This dictionary needs many hundreds more entries before we can start to translate Your Word."

Sudden Panic

"Come quick. A woman is dying!" The shout broke my mid-morning musings, and I ran out to the porch of our mud-walled house where a boy pointed across to a house on the far side of the village. I grabbed my small case of medical supplies and ran after him.

"Oh Lord," I prayed as I ran, "Please help me. I'm not a doctor. But You know all about this situation. Whatever it is, I know You can handle it."

I ran into the house and knelt down by the young woman lying flat on her back on a mat. Her mouth was closed, her nostrils were full of white foam – not breathing. I put my ear on her chest – no heartbeat. No evidence of life at all.

"She wasn't feeling well," her mother explained, "so she laid down for a nap, and suddenly she was choking, and then she stopped breathing. And after quite a while white foam came out of her nose. That's when we sent for you."

The thought suddenly popped into my head. While this girl was sleeping, she suddenly vomited and, because she was lying on her back, she breathed the contents of her stomach into her lungs. With her lungs full of stomach acid, she would have died almost instantly.

"She's gone," I said. "I can't do anything for her."

"Yes, you can!" her parents said, pointing at my medicine case. "You can give her that same injection you gave your neighbour. Remember, she died, and you brought her back to life again."

A Flashback Story

I remembered the event of a couple of months earlier. One evening Jo had gone next door to check on a girl who had been in labour nearly all day, leaving me to study by the light of the kerosene lamp. Suddenly a little girl ran in saying, "Your wife wants you to come right away."

I ran to the neighbour's house which was packed with female relatives.

"Jack," Jo said, "Her pulse is extremely fluttery and weak. For the past half hour, she has been only semi-conscious. I think she's dying."

I ran back to our house, grabbed a flashlight and scanned the contents of our medicine shelves looking for something that would help low blood pressure and a fluttery pulse. I noticed a small bottle of injectable adrenaline.

"Hmm," I thought as I grabbed the bottle and a syringe with a long needle. "Adrenaline makes the heart beat more strongly. Let's try it. There's nothing to lose." I aspirated a couple of millilitres of adrenaline into the syringe and ran back to the young mother-to-be.

She was lying very still, leaning back against her husband, barely breathing. I gave her the shot deep into a muscle mass, and felt for a pulse in her throat.

It gradually became stronger and more regular. Then suddenly, there it was, a rapid pounding heartbeat. Her eyes flew open; she took a deep breath, then another one. Relatives shouted encouragement. She pushed, let out a yell, and there was the baby! Joy all around!

What Was the Use?

No wonder this poor dead girl's parents insisted I give their daughter the same injection. So I did, knowing it would accomplish nothing for the girl, but at least I could not be accused of refusing to use the miracle injection.

I closed my medicine case, and my tears flowed freely as I joined in the crying and wailing.

And I prayed, "Lord God, I feel so helpless, so useless. There's nothing I can do but cry with them. Is that all I'm here for?"

A few hours later that prayer was answered.

~~~~~~~~~

A New Confrontation with an Old Enemy

The Husband Arrives

Other relatives joined the parents and sisters to wail and cry over the unexpected death of the lovely young woman whose life I had been unable to save. After a while, I gave my place to close relatives and stood by the door. As I saw the growing crowd outside, I realized this was a respected family, and the girl had been highly regarded as a popular singer and dancer.

Suddenly there was a commotion. The dead woman's young husband ran into the house. He had been working in his manioc plantation several kilometres away, and some friends had run back to tell him the news.

He flung himself on top of his dead wife. As he hugged her, he kept crying out, "Oh, I love you so! I love you so! Why did you have to die? I love you so!"

We all burst out crying again. The wailing went on for a long time. Eventually, some people came in with supplies to prepare her body for burial. They gently pulled her husband off his wife's body and began to paint her body decoratively and cut her hair, as if she was getting ready for a special festival.

The Last Dance

When they were done, a group of young men and women came

in. "She needs to dance with us one more time," they said.

Several young men carried her outside and held her upright while others draped her arms over the shoulders of two young men on either side of her. Then more young men and women quickly joined the line dance, singing loudly even as the tears flowed. They did the dance steps, the girl's limp legs dangling and her feet dragging on the ground. A few minutes later they carried her back into the house.

Naked Fear

Those in charge of the burial preparation wrapped her in a cloth with only her face showing, then placed her on a mat and bound it tightly all around her. At that point, two men came in with a long pole. They laid the pole on top of the bundle and tied it firmly to the pole.

Just as they lifted the pole to their shoulders and began walking toward the door, her husband stood up, his face still streaked with tears.

He shouted at his dead wife, "I used to love you! But now I don't. Now I hate you! Go away. I hate you. Don't come back here as a ghost and haunt me. I don't love you anymore. I hate you. I hate you!" Her father and mother joined in the shouting, and so did her sisters.

I stood there stunned, looking at the naked fear displayed on the faces of her family. As the burial party left, I slowly walked back home, my useless medical case hanging from my hand.

Anger and Excitement

I entered our house, sat down, and ate some dinner, and told Jo all that happened. I felt something growing within me. I was angry at Satan who had bound these people in fear of ghosts with the evil eye, returning to haunt and to kill others with a glaring look.

But I also felt a growing excitement. These people were bound with Satan's ropes of fear, but Jo and I were preparing a sharp

86

Sword of the Spirit to cut through the knots that held them bound.

It was evening, time to rest, but I was too excited to lie in my hammock to read. Instead, I sat down at my study table and continued to work on expanding that dictionary.

We *would* fill that shoebox with slips of paper! We *would* learn this language well! And, God helping us, we *would* translate the Good News that Jesus is stronger than any ghost and any spirit.

Satan Confronted

In my excitement and anger, I whispered as I worked, "Satan, I rebuke you in the Name of Jesus. You will *not* enslave these Canela people forever. These little words I learn and classify will someday declare God's Word to the Canelas in their own language. God's Word will be a sharp Sword in the Holy Spirit's Hand. He will cut through your knots and chains of fear with which you have shackled these people for generations. These slips of paper have the words that will someday declare that Jesus is the Victor over you. Jesus will cast out fear; He will build His Church and set up His Kingdom in this village."

I worked till deep into the night and could hardly wait for morning to start working again.

~~~~~~~~~~

Bible Translators Step on the Gas

People often ask me, "So, how long did it take you and Jo to translate the Bible into Canela?" I usually give the short answer, but sometimes I expand a bit.

I think back to that celebration party in the mission office basement in Brasilia, that notable day in May 1990. I stood hand in hand with a dozen colleagues from the graphic arts department circling a table.

As we sang, "Praise God from Whom all blessings flow" we looked, not at the pails of celebratory ice cream and the tall glasses of cold drinks, but at the box of 780 photo-printer-ready pages of the Canela partial Bible. We thanked God for helping us reach this major milestone and prayed for the local printer who was going to turn those pages into a thousand copies of the Holy Book.

Our work is done. I thought with relief, *I could drop dead now, and the Canelas would still get their Bible.*

During those thanksgiving prayers, my mind flashed back to another day in May, 22 years earlier, in 1968 when a veteran missionary grabbed me by the shoulder, pointed down the trail and said, "Look, Jack, see those people coming out of the jungle? Those are Canelas! They are the people you and Jo are going to be translating the Bible for!"

So "Twenty-two years" is the short answer to "How long did it take?" but it is not the honest answer.

What about the years we spent learning linguistic analysis, literacy development, and Bible translation techniques? What about the many months of traveling and casting vision in the churches and to friends and relatives to build the team of financial and prayer partners? What about the years of training in Bible school, courses in missionary medicine, short-term missions projects, and the years of pastoral work experience? Shouldn't they be counted? The more honest answer would be "It took 33 years of our lives to produce this Book."

At 33 years per translation project, no wonder it is taking so long to translate the Word of God into every living language of the world! Is there no way to speed this up?

Yes, there is!

Vision 2025

The year 1990 was a banner year. Not just because my wife and I completed that Canela partial Bible, but because 16 other people groups around the world also received the Word of God in their languages for the first time. Seventeen Bible translation projects completed in the same year was probably a record number. We were all delighted.

Yet, Bible translation planners realized that even at that accelerated rate it would take 150 years for all languages of the world to have a translation of the Bible. Seven more generations!

This was not acceptable either to Wycliffe Bible Translators, the Bible Societies, or to the churches and missionaries who partnered with us. A few years later planners set a totally over-the-top goal. They cast a vision to see a Bible translation project started in every language of the world that needs it, not in 150 years, but by the year 2025, calling it *Vision 2025*.

At this accelerated pace, the Bible translation task was simply too immense for any group, no matter how large, to do by itself. *Vision 2025*, therefore, called for developing worldwide partnerships with compatible Christian organizations and denominations. It also focused on the training and funding of nationals to translate the Bible into their own languages. The goal of all this was, of course, to empower all peoples to use Scripture, establish churches, and disciple believers while nurturing literacy, education and stronger communities.

During the last five years that my wife and I worked to complete the partial Bible translation project in Canela, about 75 new Bible translation projects began around the world. But, in one five-year period since then, 450 projects started up!

What's more, bilingual nationals, often translating into their mother tongue, staff most of these translation programs. Take, for instance, the Nawuri project in Ghana, Africa. This project started in the year 2000 with five Nawuri speakers trained, financed and responsible for accomplishing this task. So when did they expect to complete it? Did they take as long as Jo and I did? No way! They finished in only eight years!

So, Are Things Speeding Up?

Since *Vision 2025* was launched, nearly 2,000 Bible translation projects have been started, almost ten times as many as during the same time before *Vision 2025*. These new projects include communities from a few hundred to several million people. Advances in technology, infrastructure, and new approaches are speeding up the translation process. Projects such as the Nawuri are completed in half or one-third the time.

Who is doing this? Wycliffe? The scores of partner organizations? The thousands of financial partners in North America who fund these projects? The many thousands of people who pray?

No! This is God at work. He is working through all of these dedicated people and organizations as they work together, pooling their resources, knowledge, and faith.

Wycliffe's Happy Problem

Because projects are starting and completing so quickly, Wycliffe has a happy problem! The promotional and informational literature keeps going out of date! For years, Wycliffe talked about 3,000 of the world's 6,900 languages still needing Bible translation done in them. Now the 3,000 has dropped to under 1640.

This is God's doing!

We often hear "If you want to be successful and accomplish great things for God, don't ask Him to bless what you are doing, find out what God is doing and join Him in it."

Here's every believer's chance. Join Him in His work in worldwide Bible translation.

~~~~~~~~~~

The Case for Mother-tongue Translators

My wife and I traveled to Brazil 50 years ago to begin our Bible translation ministry among the Canela people. We moved into their main village, learned the language and the culture, developed an alphabet, and taught the Canelas to read, write, and do arithmetic. Then, with their help, we translated a large part of the Bible. Nearly 25 years later, we returned to Canada, leaving behind the newly-published Scriptures and a young church.

Yes, it took a very long time!

Have things ever changed since then! And not for the worse either. Praise God! The massive improvements in the world of Bible translation have been exciting, positive, and incredibly encouraging.

A Little Faster and a Lot Better

Today, for example, Bible translators are completing translation projects in indigenous languages in a much shorter time and at a smaller cost than it took to do a traditional project. And here's the icing on the cake: the quality and readability of the translation are better than ever!

How can this be? What factors are responsible for this marvelous change?

Obviously, computers play a big part. No more laborious typing, proofing and retyping. That alone saves tons of time and improves the quality immediately. So do dictionary-making computer programs and high technology communication devices.

Also, in the past three or four decades, Wycliffe Bible Translators has accumulated a wealth of firsthand knowledge about linguistics and Bible translation. The current generation of Bible translators benefit from this knowledge capital through excellent training and experienced on-the-spot consultants

The greatest reason for the exciting changes in worldwide Bible translation, however, is neither better computers nor greater knowledge, but the translators themselves.

In the past, foreigners, like my wife and I, did almost all the translations. We worked with uneducated people groups that were fluent only in their own language. Nearly all Wycliffe Bible translators faced this situation.

The Rise of the National Mother-Tongue Translator

Today, however, 80 per cent of the people groups that still need the Bible translated into their language have at least some educated people, all of whom are fluent in at least one other language besides their own mother tongue. And, what's more, often some of these educated, multilingual people are Christians. It is no wonder that God is calling more and more of these educated nationals to translate His Word into their own mother tongue. Once they are trained in Bible translation principles and techniques, funded by sponsors, and surrounded by experienced consultants, they are on the fast track to produce high-quality Bible translations.

Think of the advantages these mother-tongue translators have:

- They already know and understand both the language and the culture. It is far easier and much faster to translate accurately into one's own language than into a foreign language one has learned. (Even after twenty years, my wife and I were still finding alternate ways of saying things and discovering new things about the Canela culture.)
- They already live in the country and among the people—a vital advantage in those nations where access by foreigners is extremely difficult. (We, on the other hand, had to spend huge amounts of time and money in travel, in arranging passports, visas, and inoculations, in raising financial support on furlough, in providing special schooling for our children on the field, etc.)
- Once the translation project is completed by mother tongue translators, it is seen by the people group as something that belongs to them, not something foreign imposed from outside.
- Statistics of recently completed projects staffed by national translators show these averages: three projects in Africa and four in South Asia took an average of only 12 years to complete- about half the time it took my wife and me to complete a traditional project. The average cost per project was about 30 percent of the cost of our traditional project.

God, Wycliffe, the Church

Three essential components, besides consistent prayer, must be in place for a mother tongue Bible translation project to be successful:

- Mother tongue translators need to be gifted, prepared and called to work together as a translation committee. This is God's job.
- The translators need to be fully trained and provided with experienced consultants to help them solve translation and administrative problems and make sure the final translation is of high quality. This is Wycliffe's job.
- Financial supporters and sponsors need to fund the translation project. This is the Church's job.

Only when each of these essential components is present and functioning well, will the project move ahead to completion.

In round numbers, about 1,650 languages still do not have any part of the Bible translated into them. About one-third of these languages are spoken by people groups that are as yet uneducated and monolingual. Translation projects under these conditions need to be staffed by well-trained foreigners since no mother-tongue translators exist. Just as my wife and I did, they will use as much computer help as possible and train the indigenous speakers to help them produce an accurate and smooth flowing translation.

Approximately two-thirds of these languages, however, are spoken by people groups with at least some educated people among the population—a requirement for developing some mother tongue translators.

Current Statistics

God is mightily at work in Bible translation in the world today. Linguistic research and/or active translation is happening in 2584 languages in 170 countries.

You Version has made the Scriptures available in over 1100 languages for downloading to cell phones.

Faith Comes by Hearing has recordings of Scriptures in over 1100 languages.

The Jesus Film is available in 1500 languages,

My wife Jo and I are delighted that the Canela not only have a printed Bible but also have access to there other forms of communicating the Good News.

Many people heard God speak through Scripture in their own language for the first time this year. Trained, well-funded mother-tongue translators, assisted by experienced Wycliffe advisers and consultants, are responsible for many of these projects.

Many more projects are almost ready to start. God has gifted and called nationals to be trained and set to work, and Wycliffe is ready to train and prepare them. But for many, the start is delayed because all the needed funding is not yet in place.

National believers obviously help out where they can. They want and need the Word of God in their own language! They help build translation centres, and provide some of the locally grown food needed by the translation committees and their families. But the cost of computers, communication equipment, travel, training, and a modest salary simply cannot be provided locally. This funding must come from abroad, from individuals and churches in North America and elsewhere, just as it does to support expatriate translators who work in traditional, pioneer situations.

Before these expatriate translators leave for the field, and during each furlough, they raise the funds they need to live and work. They do this by sharing the vision with their friends, relatives, and churches in North America and inviting them to join their support team.

National translators cannot do that. They depend on third parties to raise the funding they need.

Partner groups like The Seed Company, Wycliffe Associates, and in Canada, OneBook, gather accurate information from the field, cast a clear vision to potential sponsors, handle the flow of funds and the receipting, and make sure accountability structures are in place and working well.

One of the most exciting aspects of worldwide Bible translation work is that God is calling and using trained national Bible translators to accelerate the Bible translation process in ways that we old-timers could only dream of.

~~~~~~~~~~

Para TExt: new tools for a new generation of Bible translators

Guest Article by Hart Wiens

Director of Scripture Translations, Canadian Bible Society

"I think the ParaTExt software is simply incredible. I am constantly amazed at how powerful it is, how fast it is, and how much easier it makes it to do my Bible translation project. ParaTExt is simply brilliant."

Those words from Matt and Christy Taylor, SIL translators serving in Papua New Guinea, are typical of the user response to the computer tools we deliver to translators around the world. How different is their reality to the tools we carried to our field assignment in the Philippines 40 years ago – a manual typewriter, pencils, reference books and lots of carbon paper and whiteout. We had to retype our work multiple times and used a big table for all the reference books we needed to consult. We repeatedly heard tragic stories of manuscripts being lost, burned, or eaten by termites, sometimes after years of grueling effort.

God's Gift to Accelerate Bible Translation

Today translators open their computers and on the screen they see a suite of software with multiple windows which all scroll together as they move from one verse to another. Built into our software is an entire library of Bible versions, commentaries, lexicons and other resources which they can display for use in their research even as they enter their translation in a separate window. All their work is saved on a central server in "the cloud," and they can share their work with colleagues in separate locations with the simple click of a button. If the computer is lost, stolen, or damaged, their work is still secure and can easily be recovered. The translated Scriptures are stored in a standard format which makes it relatively easy to convert the files to "typeset" page setup, ready for printing or even for immediate delivery to readers through new media such as e-books and smartphones.

God Uses His People to Develop His Gift

The software is called ParaTExt and is delivered and supported through the computer resource department of SIL, Wycliffe's field partner, and through the United Bible Societies' Institute for Computer Assisted Publishing (ICAP). The delivery and support of these tools is one of many ways in which the Bible Societies and SIL partner in the ministry of Bible translation.

SIL (Wycliffe's Field Partner) recognized the immense potential of computers to support Bible translation when it launched an ambitious project in the 1980s to produce a comprehensive suite of software to support all aspects of SIL field work. For many reasons, the project took longer than anticipated, especially for the tools to support Bible translation. Since this was a priority for the Bible Societies, UBS launched a separate project to produce a suite of tools modeled on an early prototype built by Dr. Reinier de Blois, a Bible Society consultant serving in Africa.

A Software Marriage Made in Heaven

When the first version of this program was launched in 1997, it was an immediate and unexpected hit. Very quickly the demand for this software had outstripped the capacity of the Bible Societies to support its users. For some years SIL continued to work on a parallel tool called the Translation Editor (TE), to address needs that were not covered in the early versions of ParaTExt, but the rapid development and increasing ability of

ParaTExt to meet their needs eventually resulted in an agreement to merge the two programs. This agreement to partner was due to the persistence of visionary leadership and the gracious response of SIL software development staff who set aside their tool to partner for the greater good of God's Kingdom.

Worldwide Impact

National Bible translators, many of them translating the Bible into their own mother-tongue, are effusive in their praise:

From Indonesia: Since we started using the latest version of ParaTExt our translation work became integrated and easier for our mother tongue translators and us as overseers.

From India: The ParaTExt 7 software is a great blessing and help. We wish we had known about it several years ago. That would have reduced our workload immensely.

From Georgia, Eurasia: ParaTExt provides the best translation tools ever on our computers.

From Cameroon, Africa: I want to thank you for ParaTExt 7.1. I hope to use it successfully for Bible Translation into Mfumte language.

~~~~~~~~~~

Are You Ready to Praise God for BTAKs?

"So how much have computers speeded up the work of Bible translation?" people often ask me when they find out I'm a Wycliffe Bible translator.

I'm the right guy to ask since my wife and I started our Bible translation career by handwriting the translation, then copying it with carbons on an Underwood manual typewriter. Twenty years later, it was all on a computer, and we noticed the improvement.

The big difference, however, was not in speed but in quality. Revisions were accurate since they didn't need to be typed out again, a time-intensive process that always introduced errors. Instead of hand typing and retyping three revision drafts, we now ran a Bible book through a dozen drafts, each one just a little better than the previous. The quality of the revisions greatly improved, but it still took a long time.

New Technology That Speeds Up Translation

Just a few years ago, however, a new technology was developed that really does accelerate the pace of Bible translation around the world. I'm talking about Bible Translation Acceleration Kits, also known as BTAKs, which are used by nationals translating the Bible into their own tribal languages, most of whom live in extremely isolated areas of the world.

I used to complain when my wife and I had to leave the village and drive two or three days over difficult roads to reach the translation centre in Belem where we could get our translated material checked by translation consultants. We thought we had it hard, but now I am discovering that in comparison to what some mother-tongue translators go through, we had it easy.

When I traveled in the USA raising funds for these BTAKs, my heart was stirred night after night as I watched videos of men who risk their lives getting to a translation consultant. Some travel for fifty miles across rough seas in an open boat powered by an outboard motor. Others travel for weeks over robber infested roads, climb steep mountains, or pick their way through swamps, carrying their precious manuscript to be checked at a translation centre.

For many of them, a new day has dawned. Hundreds of teams of mother-tongue translators in remote locations in Africa, Asia, and the Pacific Islands have now been equipped with Bible Translation Acceleration Kits. Even without access to electricity, phone or Internet connection, they are now communicating in real time with translation experts hundreds or even thousands of miles away via satellite connection.

So, What is a BTAK?

A BTAK consists of four main components. 1) a laptop computer, 2) a satellite communications terminal, both of which are powered by 3) an ordinary car battery which is kept charged through 4) a cloth based solar panel made of photovoltaic fabrics. It folds up into a small parcel and fits easily into a backpack along with the laptop computer, and the satellite modem. The unit is highly portable, and car batteries can be found anywhere in the world that vehicles can reach. A BTAK costs about $3,500. Although hundreds of BTAKs are already in use around the world, another 1,000 are needed immediately to meet the current demand of translators.

BTAKs: The Best Thing for Communication Since Planes

Bush planes and jungle pilots made a huge impact on missionaries sixty years ago when they began penetrating previously inaccessible areas of the world. I know. We saved weeks of travel time when we flew to and from the Canela village in Wycliffe's JAARS planes. BTAKs are the first breakthrough to accelerate the pace of Bible translation in remote areas since the start of missionary aviation.

Current high technology is a gift of God to the Church. We need to praise Him. "Thank You, Lord God of the universe, for helping Your Church to use high technology to speed Your Word to every man, woman and child on planet Earth, in their own language."

~~~~~~~~~~~

The Explosion in the Godly Software Factory

When Jo and I began working as linguist-translators among the Canela people of Brazil we did not arrive unprepared. Experienced experts had taught us how to learn an unwritten language, and Wycliffe had recommended we obtain the latest mid-1960s technology—pencils, notebooks, a manual typewriter and a high-quality reel to reel portable tape recorder.

During our first furlough, we bought a used electric typewriter and some cassette tape recorders. And that was pretty well it for most of our 22 years of working as translators. We started using the very earliest computers, using audio cassette tapes, during the late 1970s and by the time the Canela partial Bible was being prepared for printing it was all done in DOS on a computer. The disk drive was nearly the size of a washing machine, but much more expensive, and the 18-inch removable disk held 2MB of information. (Reality check: the little $10 flash drive in my pocket holds over 10,000 times the information.)

Huge Improvements in Computer Software

We all know how computer hardware systems have changed since then. But that is only the tip of the proverbial iceberg. The most profound changes affecting the areas of on-the-ground field linguistics and Bible translation have been in the area of software. Who developed this specialized Bible translation focused software? No, it wasn't Microsoft.

Currently thousands of Bible translators are using software programs to quickly and accurately compile dictionaries, analyse texts, and organize cultural data, all things our colleagues and we did by hand on little slips of paper. Today linguists analyze the sounds of an unwritten language by recording native speakers and graphing the sound visually to determine phonetic differences. We used to have to peer inside a speaker's mouth with a flashlight to see what position his tongue was in so we could replicate the sound ourselves. Who developed these marvels of technology and programming? No, it wasn't Apple either.

There is even a program that will translate a Bible book from one language into a related language producing a pretty good first draft. And believe me, it is incredibly easier, faster and better to start translating with a good first draft than with 1,000 sheets of blank paper.

And what about those hundreds of weird linguistic scripts? Scores of them are so complex, using stacked diacritics, split glyphs and contextual shaping, they could only be written by hand or laboriously typeset for printing. There was no way to type them on a computer. But now there is. Specialized word processing programs now let translators type their linguistic data, and their Bible translation on a keyboard and the symbols and scripts appear, running from right to left or from the bottom up, or from the middle in both directions, whatever the language demands.

Bible Translation Software: God at Work

So who is developing all these programs that so greatly speed up and improve Bible translations today? They are Christian men and women, gifted, trained, and called by God to give their lives to this challenging pioneer work. The work is demanding, I know. I have seen some of these folk at work—long hours, much prayer, much thought, and many studies, research, and sharing of ideas.

Nearly all of these specialists are Wycliffe members, obviously not motivated by money, but by a love for God, and a love for the hundreds of millions of people who still do not have any of God's Word translated into the language they understand best.

When I see the amazing tools available to current linguist-translators, I wish I were five decades younger. I would so join them! Oh yes!

(Editorial addition by Jack's wife, Jo, "And so would I!

Section Four: Some Inspiring Stories About Bible Translation

The Mother Who Confessed Her Secret After 22 Years

When Kathrine's baby girl was only a few days old, she did something she told no one about—not her mother, nor her sisters, not even her baby's father. She kept her action a secret for decades.

They were not easy decades. The family endured poverty—especially in the early years—faced serious illness, and suffered other pressures. When little Theodora was six years old, they moved from southern Saskatchewan to British Columbia's Okanagan Valley to start a new life. When Theodora was twelve years old, both parents were working outside the home, and she was responsible for preparing the evening meal for the family.

Although her parents didn't go to church, her mother encouraged Theodora to attend church. She did and grew up fitting in with the Christian young people who thought she was a Christian too. Then, in her early teens, after hearing a sermon on hypocrisy, she realized she needed to have a personal relationship with Jesus. She gave herself wholeheartedly to God and grew in faith and the knowledge of the Bible.

After graduating from high school, her plans to enter nurses' training fell through, and her pastor persuaded her to consider going to Bible school instead. She enrolled, enjoyed her studies and made many life-long friends, graduating with honors after three years.

She was interested in serving God overseas as a missionary and decided to take a short course in Missionary Medicine and Dentistry at the Bible Institute of Los Angeles (now Biola University). Theodora was just a few weeks short of her 22ndbirthday when Kathrine took her to the bus station for the long ride to Los Angeles. It was then that Kathrine finally confessed her secret.

"I have never told you, or anyone else," she said, "but when you were a baby, only a few days old, I dedicated you to God to be a missionary."

Kathrine went on to tell her daughter that she had prayed for her every day even before she was born, but didn't want to risk bringing any pressure on her until God Himself had led her to decide to become a missionary.

"Now that you have graduated from Bible school and are on your way to special missionary training, I thought it was right to tell you."

The following year Kathrine became my mother-in-law when Josephine Theodora became my wife.

And what a mother-in-law! Kathrine was eighteen years old and pregnant when she began praying for her baby. She prayed for her daughter right through her childhood years, her college training, her marriage, raising her three granddaughters and her ministry as a pastor's wife, and as a Bible translator.

Just a few years before the Lord took Kathrine Home to be with Him, she had the privilege of sitting next to her daughter as she distributed the newly published translation of God's Word in Canela to eager new believers.

Asked about how she felt at that time, Kathrine replied, "It was hard to have my only daughter and her family live so far away for four years at a time. I missed seeing my granddaughters grow up. I longed for them. But when I saw the joy on the faces of those Canela people as they received a Bible, it was worth it. Oh yes, it was worth it!"

Yes, Kathrine was a prayerful, loving mom, mother-in-law, and grandma.

She reminds me of a list I once saw. "Ten Success Rules for Men" I don't remember the other nine rules, but the first one was, "Marry the right woman." I would put this one next, "Have a godly mother and mother-in-law."

Happy Mothers and Mothers-in-Law Day!

~~~~~~~~~~

Five Missionary Decisions that Turned Out Well

1. God led us to choose a long-term ministry.

We knew when we left for Brazil in 1966 with our four-month-old baby and her two and three-year-old sisters, that they would be grown up before we finished the project. When we completed the multi-aspect Canela linguistic, education, medical and Bible translation program in 1990, all three had gone on to higher education, out middle daughter was married, and the other two daughters were married during the first year we were back in Canada.

A Story That Motivated Us: A tribal group, living several hundred kilometres north of the Canelas, was evangelized in the 1930s by Portuguese-speaking missionaries who made short-term visits to their villages. In the 1950s, when missions surveyors came to the area, the only evidence of Christianity they could find was one elderly tribal woman who could hum the tune of Jesus Loves Me. It wasn't until Bible translators had spent twenty years working among these people that they could sing with full understanding, "Jesus Loves Me this I know, for the Bible tells me so," because they had a Bible in their own language. Even now, twenty years later, those churches continue to spread and grow.

2. God led us to do things with the Canelas, not for them.

Right from day one, we depended on the Canela people to work with us. They taught us the language; we trained them to be translation helpers. Scores of Canela people had input into the translation. For years the envelopes we used to mail our missionary newsletters had a slogan *"Helping the Canelas Translate God's Word."*

3. God led us to train and equip Canelas so they could meet the needs of their village.

During our decades in ministry among the Canelas, we trained them in numerous ways: to dig wells for clean water, run a micro-enterprise in buying and selling, improve the stock of chickens and goats, and caring for the sick and injured. I taught a young Canela man to pull rotten teeth after I had taught myself to do it. When he became proficient, I gave him all my tools, and for the rest of my years there, he did all the dental extractions. Twenty years after we had left he was still serving his village this way. We taught a few young men and women to read and to teach others to read. By the time we left, there were scores of fluent readers, all taught by Canelas. After we left, we heard that the old chief had died. The next several chiefs chosen were all young men who had worked closely with us in literacy, translation and other projects.

4. God showed us we needed to make ourselves redundant.

When the Canelas asked us to teach them Bible stories, we determined to work ourselves out of that job as quickly as possible. On the first day, the group met I taught the first lesson, using basic teaching questions, led the discussion, and prayed over the application. On the second day, I asked one of the Canelas to teach the first lesson. When he was finished, I taught the second lesson. On the third day, one Canela volunteer taught the first lesson again, another the second lesson, and I taught the third. From then on, for seventy consecutive nights, I taught the new lesson and students volunteered to teach the previous two lessons. Twenty-five Canelas practiced teaching Bible lessons during those ten weeks.

5. God focused our work on a few things, things that would last.

We focused our efforts on leaving results that would live on long after we were dead and gone:

- An alphabet for the language
- The ability to read and write in their own language—a major stepping stone to learning the national language
- Numeracy and basic arithmetic so the Canelas would no longer be cheated in town
- A new appreciation for hygiene, soap, clean drinking water
- A sizeable portion of God's Word in their language
- An example of Christian living, in love to others, generosity, marital faithfulness, and care for our kids
- Throughout our nearly twenty-five years in Brazil, we not only prayed for the Canelas, we asked our partners at home to pray for them
- Even after the translation was complete, four-hundred prayer partners volunteered to pray for individual Canela men, women and children by name and by picture. When God moves as a result of prayer, the work lasts.

A Question.

As Jo and I pray for our families, our colleagues and our friends, we ask God to help them make decisions that will bring forth fruit—long-lasting, God-honouring results.

God led Jo and me to make these five decisions. Which ones ring a bell with you as they apply to your life?

~~~~~~~~~~

God Goes Before, and After

Bible translator's job: Translate the Bible so God can introduce Himself to people.

God's job: Prepare the people to accept the translators.

About fifty years ago, in the spring of 1968, the Canelas took the *second* step in accepting us as part of their indigenous society. My wife and I went through the Canela adoption/initiation ceremony that made us members of their families and citizens of Canela society. It involved lots of red ochre paint, plenty of tree-sap glue and white hawk down all over our bodies. Surrounded by crowds of Canelas, we listened to the chief's long speech; then each of the sub-chiefs and elders made shorter speeches.

We couldn't understand a word.

I had taken the *first* step a month earlier when I first met the Canela chief in town. Although he knew only a little Portuguese, he understood that we wanted to live in the village, learn Canela, and help where we could. He pantomimed giving me an injection in my upper arm and made writing motions. "Yes," I said, "we will treat sick people and teach you to read and write."

"You come," he said.

A few days later, I stood in the centre of the Canela village plaza surrounded by a large group of sombre, silent, serious looking Canela men. I faced a village elder who, leaning on his spear, chanted loudly for long time.

I couldn't understand a word.

Abruptly he stopped chanting, and shouted, "Prejaka! Prejaka! Prejakaaaa!" at which all those silent men behind me suddenly shouted, "Yuhaaa!"

Major adrenaline rush!

Then they all broke into smiles, grabbed my hands and kept saying "Prejaka, Prejaka, Prejaka." It finally got it! Whatever else had just happened, I now knew that I had just been given a Canela name—the *first* step into being accepted into Canela culture.

Jo and I experienced only one naming ceremony, but over the next few decades, we went through the adoption/re-initiation ceremony dozens of times—each time we returned to the village after an extended time away. And eventually we fully understood all those speeches.

"We have adopted you into our village and into our families. You are even more one of us now than when you first came to us. You now speak our language. You invented a way to write our language and taught us to read and write it and count and read numbers. You are training teachers. You make books for us. You help us with medicine. You are family and belong here. Join any festival. Go anywhere in Canela lands. Take pictures of any of us, and of any of our festivals. When outsiders come in just to look at us and our ceremonies and take pictures, we ask them for gifts, but we will never ask you."

Still true.

Some years ago, after an absence of nineteen years, (forty-one years after the original invitation), we re-visited the village. Yes, once again, glue, feathers, red paint and a wide-open village welcome to our whole family—fifteen of us—including our eight grandchildren.

God arrived in the Canela village before we came to prepare them so that they would adopt us. Then, after we left, God stayed in the village to adopt many Canelas into His Family and make them citizens in His Kingdom.

~~~~~~~~~~

Emotion, Power, and Language

I was relaxed and comfortable in the cool, breezy dining room, looking forward to some excellent food and more great conversation. I sat with my family around the laden table with our hosts, a German family who, like us, were serving as missionaries in Brazil. As we chatted, my friend leaned back in his chair and called down the hall to his teenage daughter still working in the kitchen.

Elsa! Wir sind bereit. Kommt schnell! "Elsa! We're ready. Come quickly!"

As I heard the loud voice, the urgent tone and the last word, *Schnell,* a shock of fear shot through my system and I felt the icy hand of panic clench my insides.

Terror traveled through thirty-five years of time and eight thousand kilometres of space to jab fear into my heart once again.

I was six years old, walking home from school with a classmate in Hilversum, Holland. As we took a shortcut past a warehouse, we noticed the door was partly open, so naturally, we peered in. Suddenly a German soldier carrying his machine gun ran out of a guard shack behind us shouting, *Achtung! Verschwinden Sie! Schnell!* "Hey! Get away! Quick!" I had heard those orders before, sometimes followed by shots . . . and screams.

So long ago. So far away. So many changes. I was now an adult, a husband, a father, a missionary. And this German missionary was no occupying enemy soldier—he was my friend, a missionary colleague and a brother in Jesus.

What then triggered this vivid, emotion-laden memory? Language. A specific language. The same language which had first impacted me emotionally. Had he called down that hallway in English, "Quick!!" or in Portuguese, *"Rapido!!"* I would not have reacted with such strong feelings.

Much of the power of language is in the emotion it evokes in the hearer. No wonder God used language to communicate His passionate Love letter to people. No wonder He uses thousands of languages to penetrate billions of human minds . . . and hearts. No wonder He calls hundreds of thousands of His people to work together to bring His Word to every language on earth.

Currently God's message is being translated into nearly 2,600 languages in 170 countries. But over 1,600 languages still await translator, and prayer partners, and finances.

The Church needs to listen to the urgency in His voice and get at it! *Quickly! Rapido! Rapidement! Awjarê! Szybko! Snabbt! Raskt! Gyorsan! Brzo! Schnell!*

~~~~~~~~~~

It's Enough to Make You Sick

We had been on a steep learning curve ever since we arrived

in the Canela village to learn their language and culture when suddenly the curve got even steeper.

I had hired Blackpalm, an older Canela man to help us learn his language. Every day for the previous four months, he had come to our house and patiently repeated words and phrases and corrected our pronunciation.

He always looked forward to our midmorning coffee break, and one day it was especially satisfying since Jo had made a Dutch delicacy, *oliebollen*, to go with our coffee. The doughnut-like balls were easy to make without an oven since all she needed was a pan of hot oil to deep-fry them in.

He cautiously nibbled at his *oliebol*; then his face broke into a smile as he ate it up quickly and asked for another one. All three of us ate until they were all gone. What's not to love about fried dough and icing sugar?

"How do you make these sweet things," he asked Jo.

She showed him a bag of flour and said, "This is powder made from grinding up wheat which is like rice." She then showed him the butter, milk, salt, spices, sugar, and eggs and said, "These are all mixed up into a batter, and then you drop a lump into the boiling oil, and . . . ."

"Wait!" he said, holding up his hands, "Are there eggs in these sweet things?"

When Jo said, "Yes," he jumped up, ran outside, stuck his finger down his throat, and vomited up all of Jo's delicious *oliebollen*.

When he came back, all teary-eyed, he asked, "What are you doing? Are you trying to kill my little son?"

That's when our learning curve started to go straight up as we began to research the enormous number of taboos the Canelas practice. It took years, but we eventually discovered that Canelas believe that not only what you personally eat will affect your health, but what you eat will also affect the health of close relatives. Babies, the elderly and sick people are especially vulnerable to certain foods being eaten by their relatives. There are many other ways a person can "pollute" another weaker person but eating the "polluting" types of food is the main concern.

Since it is a well-known fact among Canelas that eating eggs will cause diarrhea, and since babies are particularly prone to diarrhea and death through dehydration, no one in the immediate family eats eggs during the first year or two of a child's life. Since Blackpalm was the father of a newborn, no wonder he was so upset.

Because of this taboo, many adults don't eat eggs for 10-15 years at a stretch, denying themselves an excellent source of scarce protein. Pregnant women also tend to avoid eating meat and subsist mostly on starchy manioc root.

We prayed much and worked hard to teach Canelas the truth about health and germs and demonstrated a healthy lifestyle ourselves.

We noticed many of these taboos changing when they saw how we boiled our water and evaded many sicknesses that way. Then people learned to read and learned about hygiene and the value of clean drinking water to avoid diarrhea.

But the big changes came when early in the translation process we translated 1st Timothy. Our translation helpers' faces lit up with big smiles when they read chapter 4 verses 3-5 which taught specifically about all foods.

". . . which God created to be received with thanksgiving by those who believe and who know the truth. For everything God created is good, and nothing is to be rejected if it is received with thanksgiving because it is consecrated by the word of God and prayer."

The Canelas were a sickly group of fewer than 400 when we first started living with them in their village. By the time we left 22 years later, the village had grown to well over a thousand. Today, 50 years after the *oliebollen* incident, the village is thriving with nearly 2,500 inhabitants with healthier bodies, educated minds, and a growing number of spiritually alive souls.

Oh, yes, and the last we heard was a granddaughter of our friend Blackpalm was one of the first Canelas to finish high school and was headed for university studies to become a doctor.

As we climbed that steep learning curve Jo and I sometimes asked ourselves, "Is this going to be worth it?" We don't think that anymore!

~~~~~~~~~~

What Does It Take to Satisfy God?

For more than fifty years Jo and I have been thrilled to be members of Wycliffe Bible Translators of Canada, now a major partner—along with about eighty other likeminded organizations—of Wycliffe Global Alliance

Starting with a handful of American linguists in the 1930s, today more than 10,000 workers are focused on linguistics, literacy and Bible translation around the world. About 7,500 of these workers are European or North and South American, the other 2,500 are African, Asian, or Pacific Islanders. So what are the results?

Of the world's 7,000 living languages, about 1,300 have a New Testament or other major portions of Scripture translated into their language. About 2,200 languages have Bible translation work in progress. God is blessing and prospering His work. In the last fifteen years alone, 1,100 new Bible translation projects were started. A small percentage of the total world population, 140 million people, speaking 1,600 languages, are still waiting for a project to begin.

As a veteran Bible translator, this progress excites me. But I need to remember that cross-cultural foreign missions and Bible translation did *not* start with Wycliffe's founder Uncle Cameron Townsend in the 1930s.

Worldwide missions didn't start with Hudson Taylor's passion for China in the mid-1800s, nor with William Carey going to India in the late 1700s.

It didn't start with the apostle Paul's missionary travels to Asia and Europe. It didn't start with the arrival of the Holy Spirit in Jerusalem at Pentecost when foreigners from many nations heard the Good News in their own languages.

Foreign missions didn't even start on that mountain in Galilee when Jesus gave the disciples the Great Commission to evangelise the world and disciple the nations.

Nor did foreign missions start with the Jewish national exile to Babylon, or with Jonah, the reluctant missionary to Nineveh.

It didn't start with Solomon's dedication prayer at the temple when he asked God to hear and answer the foreigner who came from far to pray at the temple.

It didn't start during David's reign when he wrote song after song telling all the peoples of the earth to worship God.

It didn't even start with Abraham when God promised that through him, and his seed, all the nations of the earth would be blessed.

And no, it didn't start after Adam's disobedience when God promised that Satan would someday be crushed.

Foreign missions started in the great heart of God long before He made the earth and created Adam. Right from the beginning of time, God wanted every human being that was ever to live on earth to know Him.

I remember talking about this to a small audience of mature Christians in a major church. I then asked them, "But why does God want people to know Him?" I received a wide variety of answers. Acting like a two-year-old child, I kept asking, "But why?" and got an answer that was close.

"God wants to save us from our sins." Right! But why?

"He's a God of love and wants us in heaven forever." But why?

Finally, one lady gave the right answer,

"So we can worship Him in Spirit and in Truth forever." Right!

Almighty God wants everyone to enthusiastically admire Him,

deeply respect Him, tell Him over and over again how great, how powerful, and how perfect He is. The time is coming when we will all obey the first of the Ten Commandments in the way God Himself obeys it ¾ to love and worship the Lord God and Him alone. At last, we will delight in God's perfection in the same way He delights in His own perfection.

John Piper says it well in his book, *Let the Nations be Glad!* "Missions exists because worship doesn't."

Ultimately Wycliffe and all missions are not about people at all; they are about God¾ God who is to be freely and exuberantly worshipped in thought and word, in song and deed, in life and death.

What about those 1,600 languages without any of God's Word yet translated into them. Do any of those 140 million speakers know God?

Wycliffe and the work of Bible translation must continue to grow until God is praised and worshiped in every one of those languages.

Remember the story of the ninety-nine sheep safely in the fold and the shepherd going out to find the one lost sheep?

I suspect that God will not be satisfied until He hears people from every single language on earth worshiping Him.

~~~~~~~~~~~

The Book of Heaven

David Thompson is well-known in western Canada as the mapmaker who explored that part of North America 200 years ago. What is not as well-known is that, as a devout Christian, he carried his Bible and told stories about Jesus and heaven everywhere he went. In 1807, while charting the homelands of the Flathead Salish people who lived in southern Alberta and northern Montana, he found that these people couldn't get enough of his stories. "Someday, someone will come and bring you the 'Book of Heaven'" he told them.

In 1832, a whole generation later, the tribe could wait no longer and sent four men on a 5,000-kilometre round trip to St. Louis, Missouri to find the Book and bring it back. Two of the men died before they arrived. The remaining two were received at the fort by General William Clark of the Lewis and Clark expedition who introduced them to a priest.

The two emissaries, however, were disappointed when no one could give them the Book of Heaven. Just before they started on their return journey, the town put on a farewell feast complete with many speeches. At the end of the feast, one of the Salish envoys gave a speech that had far-reaching consequences.

"We came to you over the trail of many moons from the land of the setting sun beyond the great mountains ... we came with an eye partly open for our people who sit in darkness; we go back with our eyes closed.

"We made our way to you with strong arms through many enemies and strange lands, that we might carry back much to them. We go back with our arms empty. Our people sent us to get the white man's Book of Heaven. You took us where they worship the Great Spirit with candles, but the Book was not there. You showed us images of the good spirits and pictures of the good land beyond, but the Book was not among them to tell us the way.

"We are going back the long, sad trail to our people of the dark land. You make our feet heavy with gifts, and our moccasins will grow old, and our arms tire in carrying them, yet the Book is not among them. When, after one more snow, we tell our people in the big council that we did not bring the Book, no word will be spoken by our elders or our young men. One by one they will go out in silence. Our people will die in darkness. They will have no white man's Book to make the way plain. I have no more words."

As news of this speech spread among Christians in England and the north-eastern US, missionaries and Bible translators began to penetrate the west. The Bible was translated into Cree

25 year later, but it would be many generations before the Flathead-Salish finally received the Book of Heaven in their own language.

Currently, almost 7,000 languages are spoken by the world's 7.6 billion people. An estimated 141 million people speak 1,636 languages in which not even one line of the Bible has yet been translated. Like the Flathead-Salish people of 200 years ago, they wait and wait.

Translating the Book of Heaven into these 1,636 languages is not a peripheral option—it is the most foundational task left for the Christian Church to accomplish.

~~~~~~~~~~

What's so Fascinating about Bible Translation?

A few years ago a lady stopped me on the way out of church and said, "Hey, I heard your interview on the radio yesterday. You did a great job answering those questions! It was fascinating." (And she wasn't even my Mom!)

I thanked her, chatted a bit, and drove home wondering, "What is so fascinating?" I had simply answered some questions about Bible translation, linguistics, and literacy, and tossed in a few personal anecdotes. What's so fascinating about that?

The Rotarian and the Translator

As I thought about it, I remembered the time I was crawling on the floor of a hotel dining room, taping down the power cables for our fundraising and recruiting banquet that evening. A Rotary lunch meeting had just ended, and the president of the Rotary club was chatting with our banquet tour director. The Rotarian walked over to me and asked, "I hear you learned a Brazilian indigenous language from scratch. No books, no teachers. Is that right?"

I stood up, glad for the chance to straighten my back, and said, "Yes, my wife and I worked in a translation project for twenty-two years." The president was full of questions and kept looking at me in wonder as I told him about pulling teeth and doing other medical work, learning the language and the culture, developing an alphabet, making up learn-to-read primers, training literacy teachers, translating the Bible, and training Bible teachers. He could not get enough of it.

Suddenly he glanced at his watch and said, "Look, I've got to get back to work. But, uh, um, would you mind if I shook your hand? I've never met anybody like you." I blinked in surprise, then I shook hands with him, and he walked away, looking back one more time from the doorway.

As I knelt to tape down another section of cable, I looked at my hand thinking, *The guy is right. Translators' hands really are special, but we just don't realize it. On the field, most of my friends were translators too. We got used to the extraordinary nature of our work. What was routine and common to us is exotic and fascinating to others.*

In the past ten years, however, the colour of translators' hands has darkened, and I do not mean with age spots! Increasingly the fingers on the translator's keyboard are not white like mine, but black and brown—the fingers of dedicated and talented nationals, gifted and called by God to translate His Word into their own indigenous languages. They often work in committees, surrounded by Wycliffe trained facilitators— veteran translators who train them and consult with them as they work.

Peter's Story

Peter is a native of a West African country who grew up in a village that spoke only the tribal language. His parents and the village elders noticed that he was unusually bright and quick to learn in the village school. Eventually, a government school inspector chose Peter to come with him to the city and attend a school taught in the national language. He became a Christian while studying the Bible and eventually graduated with a degree in education.

Years later, when he was a tenured teacher with a guaranteed salary, he felt God urging him to translate the Scriptures into his own tribal language. He resigned his teaching position to head up a Bible translation committee. The national translators received a modest salary through funding generated by foreign Wycliffe affiliated organizations. Eight years later, they completed the translation in their own language.

National translation committees like Peter's are working all over the world. They are great models of interdependent partnerships—translators contributing the profound knowledge of their native culture and language, with experienced Wycliffe consultants from many countries providing their expertise in linguistics, literacy, translation techniques, and in biblical culture and language. Meanwhile, in North America, thousands of people are praying for these national translation committees and funding the programs through their gifts.

Out of the over 1600 languages that still need to have a Bible translation program started, trained and gifted bilingual nationals could probably handle about two-thirds of these translation projects. They often work in cluster projects of different, but related languages, helping each other to solve translation problems common to their languages. Compared to a traditional, expatriate staffed team working under monolingual conditions, these national committees often complete a translation in half the time and at half the cost.

Never before in the history of the world have there been so many Bible translation projects going on at the same time. The rate at which new translation projects are being started is increasing. The Holy Spirit is up to something wonderful.

God is at work. Now *that* is fascinating!

~~~~~~~~~~

Learning to Follow God

The computer operators and the programmers at the mission centre in Belem, Brazil, heaved a huge sigh of relief when Jack the Jerk and his family finally left on a mini-furlough. They'd had enough Popjes Pressure to last them for the rest of the year.

For weeks I had asked and insisted, pressured and persisted, straining relationships with my coworkers with my haste, until at last, the line printer spat out a first draft translation of Luke and Acts in Canela. (Printing the seventeen Canela vowel symbols was a complex process in the late 1970s.)

I addressed the parcel to Jaco, our best translation helper, and gave it to a friend who assured me he would give it to the government agent in the village to pass on to Jaco.

During our brief visit to Canada, I excitedly told our prayer and financial partners, "A first draft copy of Luke and Acts is now in the Canela village and is being read. Pray that God will reveal Himself to the readers."

Several months later, we returned to Brazil and found that Brazil's anti-missionary policies were still keeping us out of the Canela village. It was another full year before we managed to arrange a visit with Jaco in a small Brazilian town outside of Canela land. We were delighted to see him arrive with notes and gifts from Canela friends.

One gift parcel looked familiar, and I realized it was wrapped in the same paper I had used to wrap the Luke and Acts printout. Opening the parcel was like being punched in the stomach. There was the Scripture printout! Still as clean, new, and unread, as it was when I wrapped it nearly two years before.

Jaco was astonished! "This parcel has been lying on the desk of the government agent in the village for over a year. I saw it there. He gave it to me to give to you. Why didn't he give it to me? Look, it has my name on the front!"

I couldn't answer his question and had some of my own. "Hadn't I worked hard and long to translate, print, and move those books nearly 1,000 kilometres into the village? Then why didn't God move that parcel one arm's length from the agent's desk to Jaco's hand?"

The answer came eventually: God seems to have a schedule,

a timetable. He waits until everything is ready, then acts instantly and decisively. God's character or "brand" knows nothing of frantic haste or hurry. Rather, He schedules His activities, doing things at the right time by His agenda.

I had heard testimonies of how people had "hit bottom" in their addiction before they saw they needed God. Was it possible that the Canela society simply was not yet ready to turn to God? That the Canelas needed to "hit bottom" before they saw Jesus as their Saviour?

I was slowly getting my head around the concept that to God, Sooner is not better than Later, nor is Faster better than Slower, but that there will come a moment when He will act.

I felt ashamed as I thought about what a jerk I had been, pushing my coworkers in Belem to work around the clock to get that printout done. I had damaged relationships in my desperate hurry to get God's Word into the village. Now I realized I had been faster than God! I was not following God, I was trying to lead Him. How absurd!

I should have remembered and believed the passage in Isaiah 60:22 where God promises to do something for Israel after the nation had waited a long time. "I am the Lord, in its time I will do this swiftly" (NIV).

When Jaco left to return he carried with him that same parcel of printouts eager to read the stories one after another.

~~~~~~~~~~

Missionaries Living in Dangerous Situations

For the past weeks, the TV news has been showing refugee men and women and children fleeing their war-torn countries. The heart-rending scenes of desperate families, exhausted children, worried mothers and frustrated fathers risking their lives and sometimes losing them while trying to escape danger and death reminded me of a story I heard about one of our Wycliffe missionaries.

120

Dangerous Mission Fields

He and his family were living in Colombia during an especially dangerous time. One Wycliffe missionary had already been kidnapped and killed while others were threatened by the terrorist drug gangs because of Wycliffe's work with indigenous people in the jungle.

When this family came home on furlough, someone asked him,

"When did you first realize that you were living in a dangerous situation?"

He thought for a minute and then told this story:

The Story

Our family lives in Loma Linda, and we had gotten used to hearing nightly gunfire. One evening, as I took my young son to his bedroom and tucked him into bed, I noticed that none of his teddy bears were in bed with him. They were all lined up on the dresser along the wall between the window and the bed. So I asked him,

"Which teddy bears would you like to sleep with tonight?"

"None of them, Daddy. I want them all to sit there on the dresser."

I said, "Okay," and prayed with him, then kissed him goodnight and turned to leave. As I was opening the door, I heard his little voice call,

"Daddy!"

"Yes?"

"Daddy, if a bullet comes through the window and goes through all my teddy bears, will it still kill me?"

That's when it hit me. We were living in a dangerous location!

Restricted Access Countries

This missionary family is not the only one who live and work and raise their families in perilous places. Many mission agencies, including Wycliffe and its field partner organizations, have workers in what are called restricted access countries.

Although they are legal residents of the country with full authority from the government to do their work, there are terrorist groups that would kill them if they knew what they were doing. So they live under assumed names, can't have a website, a blog, or a Facebook page. They can't even tell their supporting partners the name of the country in which they live and work.

A Closing Story

In the last century, a missionary named James Calvert led a group to work among the cannibals of the Fiji Islands. The ship captain tried to turn him back, saying,

"You will lose your life, and the lives of those with you, if you go among such savages."

"We died before we came here," James responded.

That's the very attitude today's missionaries have when they travel to live and work in these dangerous situations.

~~~~~~~~~~

It's a New One!

Scene 1: 1981, in North America

In churches, prayer meetings, Sunday schools, and homes, tens of thousands of people pray for the thirty-three hundred people groups around the world that still do not have even one passage of Scripture translated into their own language:

"Send out Bible translators. Raise up financial supporters. Open doors to these people groups. Speak to hearts through Your Word as it is translated. Bring these people groups into your Kingdom."

Scene 2: 1981, a translation centre in Belem, Brazil

Twenty Bible translators pray earnestly for a dozen people groups in their area:

"Please open the way for us to return to the villages. It's been three years since we have had any contact with them. Oh, God, we miss them so! Change the government policy that forbids us to visit these villages. In the meantime, prepare the hearts of the Apalai, the Apinaje, the Canela, and the other people groups to obey the small portions of Your Word that have been translated."

Scene 3: 1981, a Canela village in Brazil

Jaco, a young man, swings in his hammock in a palm thatch house. He is reading a pack of stapled pages, a print out of the first draft of the books of Luke and Acts. After a while, he puts the papers down and begins to talk to himself.

"I've been reading these pages every day for many months. Three years ago, I helped to translate them. When am I going to stop just reading them? When will I believe them, and obey them?"

He climbs out of the hammock, walks out to the backyard, and looks up into the clear blue sky and says,

"*Cojkwa kam Inxu cati*—Great Father in the sky—This is me, my name is Jaco. You don't know me, but I've been reading Your papers, and according to them I am bad, very bad. I am sorry. Please don't remember my badness. Please do something for me and help me to live right from now on."

Scene 4: 1981, Heaven

The usual multitude of angels is singing and praising God around His throne. A large number of angels lean over the parapets of heaven to observe the people on earth. Suddenly one of the angelic watchers holds up both hands and shouts, "Stop! Listen!"

Heaven falls silent as the angels listen intently. They hear a voice from earth, "*Cojkwa kam Inxu cati* . . .

The angels look at each other astonished. "We've never heard that language here before. This is not just a repentant sinner. It's a new one—the first one in his people group!"

Instantly a swelling cheer of joy resounds throughout heaven! Thousands more angels, whole choirs of them, come flying from every part of heaven carrying their instruments with them. A musical extravaganza of overwhelming joy begins.

In the scribe room, the recording angel checks his list, makes a mark alongside "Canela" and says, "Three-thousand, two-hundred and ninety-nine to go."

2018 Update

Since 1981, the angelic choirs have heard words of repentance in more than a thousand languages never before heard in heaven. They are celebrating with joyful musical extravaganzas more often than ever before in the history of the world.

The recording angel checks off names at an accelerating pace. Currently, on his 7,000-name list of nations, ethnic groups, and languages, about 1,636 remain.

May God's people on earth keep praying fervently, keep giving generously, and keep volunteering their lives to translate the Good News into every single language in the world.

~~~~~~~~~~

Bible Translators' Biggest Challenge: Part One

The interviewer introduced me to his radio audience, asked me to describe the work that Wycliffe does, and then asked, "What are the biggest challenges facing Bible translators today?"

I'm not usually stumped since I'm often interviewed when on Wycliffe Associates banquet speaking trips. This question, however, was not an easy one to answer.

If you asked several pastors, "What are the biggest challenges facing pastors in North America today?" you would get a wide variety of answers, even though the similarities among churches greatly outnumber the differences.

But the differences among translation programs are enormous. There simply is no "typical" translation program.

I told the interviewer that currently, Bible translators are working in nearly 2,200 languages in more than 130 countries.

Varieties of Bible Translation Programs

1. Some of these translation programs are staffed by expatriate linguist/translators working together with nationals who have little or no education, speak only their own language and have no idea what the Bible is about. These are examples of the extreme pioneer conditions under which my wife and I translated a partial Bible in Brazil. Other programs are staffed by expatriate trainers and consultants who work together with educated, multilingual Christian nationals who are translating into their own mother tongue. Obviously the challenges faced by translators in these two utterly different types of programs are poles apart.

2. Some translators work in languages which have never been written; others work in communities that have a long tradition of literacy in their own language.

3. Some translators work in isolated valleys, or distant islands, or in inhospitable regions of the world where there are no physical amenities like clean water, electric power, easy communications or transportation. Others work in or near cities where all these services are taken for granted.

4. Some translators work in areas of the world where the Bible is appreciated and respected, while others work in countries dominated by non-Christian world religions with adherents that are strongly antagonistic to any religion other than their own.

5. Some translators work right in their co-translators' community; others work with co-translators who are living outside their country.

6. Some translators work face to face with their co-translators, others work via email and Skype communications.

These are just a half a dozen differences, and they can come in a wide variety of combinations. No wonder the challenges facing Bible translators on the field differ so much.

There is one challenge all Bible translators have in common, however, and that is that they need to be supported spiritually in prayer, and financially by churches and friends at home on whose behalf they work at this ministry.

~~~~~~~~~~

Five Reasons Why the Church Might Not Keep on Supporting Bible Translation

Bible Translation Challenge: Part Two

In the previous article, I listed half a dozen different situations under which Bible translators work. Since these situations can be combined in scores of ways, each Bible translation project has its own unique challenge. One challenge all Bible translators have in common, however, is the need to be supported spiritually, and financially by churches and friends on whose behalf they work at this ministry.

1) Decreasing Interest in Reading the Bible Among Churches and Individual Christians

A recent Angus Reid survey of Canadians shows that Christians of all traditions are reading the Bible much less compared to 18 years ago. Even evangelicals, who most strongly believe that the Bible is the Word of God, are studying the Bible less. Check out the illustrated report or download it from this site. http://www.bibleengagementstudy.ca/

126

Not Reading the Bible is Putting God's Word in Chains.

It appears that churches and individual Christians, including Bible-believing evangelicals, are less and less convinced of the reliability, relevance, trustworthiness and divine origin of the Bible. As a result, a smaller percentage of Christians are reading Bible, and even those who are reading God's Word, are reading it less. If this trend continues, it will no doubt have a negative impact worldwide Bible translation. After all, why would a Christian who rarely reads his own Bible, pray for and give money to far away Bible translation projects?

2) Ignorance of the Strategic and Critical Importance of Bible Translation

Many churches simply are not interested in learning about "yet another critical worldwide missions need." They already have their own denominational mission agencies and are involved in prayer and giving in their own missions programs. They simply can't fit yet another worthy ministry into their budget.

What such churches do not understand is that providing the Bible in every language spoken on earth is essential to fulfilling God's plan for world evangelization. How else can Christ's Church be made up of "some from every tribe and language and nation?" Revelation 7:9

3) Churches Are Happy with 97%: But God Wants 100%

Churches are happy to know that 97% of the world's population speak languages in which at least some part of the Bible has been translated, or in which translators are currently working. Many churches look at the big picture and feel that 97% is a good "market share."

They need to remember Jesus' parable about the ninety-nine sheep safely in the sheepfold, and the shepherd's anxiety about the one lost sheep. Jesus is concerned about the 3% of the world's people who are lost in cultural gullies and tangled in linguistic thickets that keep them from hearing His saving Word.

4) Churches Have No Idea How Complex Bible Translation Is.

Pastors and church leaders, in general, have no idea how incredibly complex the Bible translation task is. Not only does it need to be translated into a language which is utterly different from English, Greek or Hebrew, but also into an exotic indigenous culture.

Pastors sometimes translate a passage from biblical Greek into modern English. In comparison to the challenges faced daily by the translators on the field, such an exercise is kindergarten stuff—mere child's play.

5) Churches Don't Realize Christianity is a Translated Religion

Most Christians, including pastors and church leaders, do not realize that Christianity is a "translated religion." That is, historically the Christian faith has only ever spread successfully and healthily where the people had a translation of the Bible in their own language and culture.

In the first three centuries, the North African church flourished, producing great theologians such as Tertullian, Cyprian, and Augustine. But with the rise of Islam, the Christian Church disappeared completely. Historians tell us the main reason was that the North African Church never translated the Bible into the indigenous, Berber and Punic languages, and their cultures. Instead, Latin language and culture were taught to believers along with the Christian Faith.

In contrast, during that same time, in Egypt and Ethiopia, the Bible was translated into the Coptic and Ethiopian indigenous languages. As a result, Christianity survived the rise of Islam.

The worldwide Church still needs to complete the Great Commission to evangelize the world. This can only be done by translating the Good News into every language spoken on earth. Over 1,900 to go.

The Biggest Challenge Translators Face

The biggest challenge facing Bible translators is, therefore, how to get and keep, the Church in the homeland solidly behind them spiritually and financially.

~~~~~~~~~~

Can You Explain These Coincidences Without Getting Theological?

In 1983, thirty-four years ago, a group of 40,000 Sudanese people called the Tira did not have a single word of the Bible translated into their language. Today, and for the past fifteen years, thousands of Tira people are reading the Bible in their own language and have turned to follow God.

How did that happen?

- In November of 1983, David and Ray, two American students signed up to pray for the Tira with Wycliffe's Bibleless Peoples Prayer Project.

- In May of 1986, Jerry and Jan promised to pray for this group.

- In March 1990, Jane and Margeanne committed themselves to pray.

In August 1990, a report came to the Prayer Project organizers that Avajani—a young Christian Tira man—was studying linguistics and Bible translation techniques. The organizers wrote to encourage him with the news that three teams were praying for his Tira people. They gave the names and the dates when they began to pray. Avajani's response was astonishing! Here's what he wrote:

- I became a Christian in November 1983, the month David and Ray began to pray.

- I was accepted for theological studies in May 1986, when Jerry and Jan started to pray.

- I heard about courses in Bible translation and was accepted as a student in March 1990, when Jane and Margeanne started to pray.

After his training, he began translating, and some portions of the Bible were published during 1999-2001.

An atheist reading this sort of astounding coincidence might well mutter to himself, "Hmm, if I didn't know any better, I'd think that God was involved."

God is definitely at work on planet Earth, and He invites us to join Him by praying. God has limited Himself to work on earth only in response to the prayers of His people. That is why every work of God is preceded by prayer. He moves some to pray, and some to work with their hands and minds. At rock bottom, He wants every person on earth to hear about Him in the language they know best.

Here are some links to help us join God in His work:

www.wycliffe.org/prayer

www.ethnologue.com/world

~~~~~~~~~~

How God Stamped His Word "Holy" to the Canela

The Problem

Each time I told a story to the Canelas about Jesus performing a miracle they told me a story of the great exploits of some Canela culture heroes from their legends and myths. We tried to tell them that the stories from the Bible were special, true, real, and unique. They were Holy, having to do with God. They didn't get it. We prayed – a lot.

Then it got worse. The Brazilian government changed, and the new officials refused to renew the permissions missionaries needed to live and work among indigenous peoples We found ourselves exiled from the Canela village. We prayed – a lot.

The Permit

We kept on working on the mission centre in the city, completing seven easy-reading booklets and the books of Luke and 1&2 Thessalonians. When the newly printed books arrived, we made a formal request to the government to visit the village and deliver the nine books. We prayed – a lot.

We praised God when we received a notice that permission had been granted but with exceptions. I flew to Sao Luis to see the government official. He gave me the permit and asked me to read it. I noticed that although we were allowed to leave the seven reading booklets in the village, the books of Luke and 1&2 Thessalonians were excluded. I had to sign a promise that I would not leave the books of sacred Scripture in the village.

I took my pen, shot up a prayer to God to work this out in His own way, and signed the document. On my return to the centre I told my missionary colleagues, and we prayed – a lot.

The Excitement

The next day, John, a fellow missionary, and I loaded a steel drum with seventy sets of books packed in plastic bags onto his pickup truck and left for the Canela. Several days later the Canelas received us with great joy since it had been several years since we were there. Their joy turned into wild excitement when they saw the seventy-five parcels of nine books in their language. The chief and elders immediately ordered me to the village central plaza and report.

I showed them each of the seven reading books. The elders were pleased to see several of their favourite legends in print as well as the health and hygiene booklets. When I finished, the chief pointed to the two remaining books, the Scripture books. "What about those books?" he asked.

"Oh, those are different. I can't leave them here."

"Why not? What are they about?"

"One is about Jesus, the Son of God when He lived on earth long ago. And the other is the counsel of Paul. He was one of the elders of the Jesus group."

"Well, you can at least tell us what is in those books," the chief said.

The Explanation

So, for the next hour I gave an overview of the life of Jesus, reading excerpts from Luke, then read parts of Paul's letter.

"We really want those books!" the chief exclaimed, "Why can't you leave them?"

I explained about the government permission and that I had promised not to leave the Bible books. "I will leave them with my friend Sr. Duca in town," I said, "You can go there and pick them up and bring them in yourselves."

The Canela elders were not pleased with that idea at all. "It's seventy kilometres to town," they said, "it's a two-day walk and two days back.

"Do those government people have these stories in their language?" the chief asked.

"Yes, they have. These stories about Jesus were translated into Portuguese hundreds of years ago. All Brazilians have been able to read them for many generations."

"Then, why won't they let us have them?" the chief exclaimed. "Why can't we read those books and choose for ourselves if we want them or not? They did!"

"Just leave them here," one of the elders advised, "We won't tell anyone you did."

"No, I'm sorry, I can't do that," I said, showing them my copy of the document, "I promised the government chief that I would not leave them here and signed his paper."

The Chief's Anger

Suddenly the chief sprang up, pulling his machete from its sheath. He laid the sharp edge on his forearm, and, with his face inches from mine, shouted, "If I cut my arm what comes out? Blue stuff? No! Red blood. We Canelas are human beings just like those city people! Why do they treat us as if we aren't people? Why can't we have what they have had for a long time?"

I couldn't answer, and we sat quietly for a while. Suddenly the chief said, "The counsel will talk about this some more, and in the morning, we'll tell you what we have decided." So, John and I went to our house in the village, and we prayed – a lot.

At sunrise, on the central plaza, the chief gave us his orders. "Put all those books back into that steel drum. Load it onto your truck and drive back up the road twenty kilometres through the gate where the Indian land ends. My son will follow you on the government tractor. He will bring the drum back on the tractor and distribute the books. That way you have kept your promise to the government, but our seventy readers will have all the books."

God's Solution

And that's what was done. We heard later that the first books everyone wanted to read were, of course, the special books, the forbidden ones. Our prayers were answered!

It was a clear example of Psalm 76:10, "Surely the wrath of man shall praise thee." when God used the government's prohibition to draw attention to the uniqueness of His Word. From then on, the Canelas treated the Bible stories as special, true and unique.

When, ten years later, the partial Bible was published it was called, *Pahpam Jarkwa Cupahti Jo Kahhoc.* **The Book of God's Highly Respected Word**

133

About the Author: Jack Popjes

Jack and his wife, Josephine

Jack has taught classes and told stories, preached in churches and spoken at events at least 1,500 times in over 20 countries in every continent except Antarctica. (He is still hoping for an invitation from the Penguin Mission Society.) He has spoken in nearly 500 cities from Albuquerque to Amsterdam, Brasilia to Bridgetown, Castries to Calgary, and so on through the alphabet, ending in Winnipeg to Willemstad, York to Yreka, and Zanderij to Zeeland.

Jack is as much at home wearing a suit, outlining a proposal in an executive boardroom as sitting half-naked by a smoky campfire swapping stories with illiterate, indigenous jungle villagers.

Jack has several "chief claims to fame." He and Jo, the "wife of his youth", have been married for 55 years. They have three daughters, three sons-in-law and eight grandchildren who love them and each other. As if that is not enough, they also lived and worked in Brazil for 24 years as linguists, educators, and Bible translators.

When they accepted the invitation to live among the Canela, there was no approved alphabet, and not one verse of the Bible had been translated into the Canela language. When they left 22 years later, scores of adults could read and write in Canela, a bilingual education program had been set up, some adults could read Portuguese, a 750-page partial Bible—Old

Testament portions and the New Testament—had been translated and published, and there were Bible-reading new believers in every extended family.

Jack began writing a weekly blog in 1995, long before the word was invented, sending out his brief story-based essays and reports to 1,400 friends and colleagues on his email list. Many of his postings were forwarded, reprinted in magazines and translated into other languages. Wycliffe USA eventually asked him to send them a collection of the best columns to be published in a book for a wider audience. That book, *A Poke in the Ribs* sold so well it was soon followed by *A Kick in the Pants*, and then *A Bonk on the Head*. In 2012 he published his first ebook, *A Tickle on the Funny Bone*, a collection of his humour columns that include his infamous April Fool's tricks.

Connect with the Author

Email: jack_popjes@wycliffe.ca

INsights & OUTbursts blog: http://www.jackpopjes.com

Twitter: @JackPopjes: https://twitter.com/JackPopjes

All the articles in this book were written as blog posts. Ten of the total fifty-two articles were taken from the author's previously published printed books:

A Poke in the Ribs; Available on Amazon.com and Amazon.ca

A Kick in the Pants; A Bonk on the Head; Available from the Wycliffe Canada bookstore in Calgary, AB, the Wycliffe USA bookstore in Orlando, FL, or, even better, autographed by Jack, directly from the author via email or Jack's blog.

Made in the USA
San Bernardino, CA
28 July 2018